Joan Marble was a member of the Rome Garden Club and the Foreign Journalists' Association in Rome. Born in Boston and educated at Smith College, she wrote her first published article about the Rose Garden at the White House. Her previous book, *Notes from an Italian Garden*, told of how she created a garden in the hamlet of Canale just north of Rome. She and her husband divided their time between Rome, Canale and London before her death in Spring 2004.

Also by Joan Marble

NOTES FROM AN ITALIAN GARDEN

IN DEFENSE OF HOMO SAPIENS
(written as Joan Marble Cook)

Notes from a Roman Terrace

JOAN MARBLE

Illustrated by Corinna Sargood

BLACK SWAN

NOTES FROM A ROMAN TERRACE
A BLACK SWAN BOOK: 0 552 77108 2

Originally published in Great Britain by Doubleday,
a division of Transworld Publishers

PRINTING HISTORY
Doubleday edition published 2003
Black Swan edition published 2004

3 5 7 9 10 8 6 4 2

Set in 11/14pt Melior by
Falcon Oast Graphic Art Ltd.

Black Swan Books are published by Transworld Publishers,
61–63 Uxbridge Road, London W5 5SA,
a division of The Random House Group Ltd,
in Australia by Random House Australia (Pty) Ltd,
20 Alfred Street, Milsons Point, Sydney, NSW 2061, Australia,
in New Zealand by Random House New Zealand Ltd,
18 Poland Road, Glenfield, Auckland 10, New Zealand
and in South Africa by Random House (Pty) Ltd,
Endulini, 5a Jubilee Road, Parktown 2193, South Africa.

Printed and bound in Great Britain by
Cox & Wyman Ltd, Reading, Berkshire.

Papers used by Transworld Publishers are natural, recyclable
products made from wood grown in sustainable forests. The
manufacturing processes conform to the environmental
regulations of the country of origin.

To dear Robert

Contents

III CIRCENSES – CIRCUSES

Illustrations

Notes from a Roman Terrace

I

PANEM – BREAD

Our flat

~

Our palazzo

~

Our neighbourhood

~

Our daily bread

While working on this book about Rome, I have often had the sensation that I was living in the age of Marcus Aurelius. Although he died in AD 180, many of the customs and special mindsets that flourished in those distant times are still alive and well in the capital city today. There is a kind of seamless continuity which persuades me that many of the qualities that are part of the contemporary Roman psyche were implanted in DNA codes thousands of years ago. The most obvious relics of Rome's past glory are the visual ones that I see every day as I move about the city. But it isn't just the buildings and the cobblestones that remind me of ancient Rome. It is the people themselves and the whole web of social, political and family arrangements that seem to me to have survived intact from the second century AD.

Unlike most of the great cities of the world, Rome was never involved in manufacturing. It was the capital of the greatest empire in the ancient world and its prosperity resulted entirely from the spoils of war. All the citizens of Rome, rich and poor, were dependent upon the empire to support them. To maintain this giant empire, the city developed an upper class of law-makers, administrators, engineers and generals whose main job was to preserve Roman supremacy. Eventually it was the generals who found their way to the top, promoting themselves to the rank of emperor. Some, such as Augustus, were worshipped as gods. Using slave labour, they built magnificent public buildings and triumphal arches as well as eight bridges across the Tiber and one thousand public baths, some of which would accommodate nine thousand citizens a day.

This public display of wealth, however, does not hide the fact that there was a huge gap between the ruling classes and the masses. Some of the cleverest members of the lower classes attached themselves to the coat-tails of leading citizens, who rewarded them with handouts and minor jobs in the administrative offices. I suspect that this marked the beginning of the system of clientelismo (patronage) still prevalent in Rome today, and found in every lacklustre bureaucracy in the city, from the Post Office to the police service. It may also have triggered the widespread Roman belief that all they have to do is sit around and complain and the state will take care of them.

Nevertheless, with the growth of the empire and the influx of citizens from even its furthest reaches, the lower orders became restless, and in an attempt to quiet them the government agreed that they should be given a regular weekly handout of grain. To ensure that the grain supply kept flowing into Rome, the emperors had to maintain steady pressure on the outlying provinces. It was reported that Spain and Egypt were required to increase their wheat shipments even when their own people were starving. The Italian government today still has laws to enable the poor to buy bread at reasonable prices, and the humble loaf remains the staple of many a family diet. The second most common items on the tables of the poor are spaghetti and pizza, both of them inexpensive first cousins of bread.

Another stratagem that the emperors adopted to keep the masses in line was to organize gladiatorial shows where the citizens were admitted free. When Titus inaugurated the Colosseum, five thousand beasts were killed within a hundred days, and many of the gladiatorial fights were arranged so that none of the fighters could escape alive. Sometimes condemned criminals were dropped into the cages of elephants and tigers to be mauled to death. Although the crowds loved the spectacles, Suetonius reports that many of the Vestal Virgins, who had special seats near the emperor, had to be carried out fainting in shock.

The poet Juvenal found the whole scene degrading. 'The people that once bestowed commands and consulships . . . now meddle no more, and long eagerly for just two things – bread and circuses,' he wrote.

I have chosen to structure this book around Juvenal's idea of 'bread and circuses'. The first section will deal with the bread itself, and also attempt to cast some light on the joys and frustrations of setting up home (and a terrace) in an ill-equipped Roman palazzo. The second section will describe some of the people we have known during our long stay in Rome, including friends who have shared our enthusiasm for ecology and gardening. The third section of the book will take a hard look at some of the circuses that now play a prominent role in Roman life. These chapters will stress the importance of television in building up the circus craze. Indeed, the glowing box has taken the place of the glowing hearth in most homes: TV has become Italy's new preacher, peep show, sports stadium, political forum and daily newspaper (with half the space devoted to advertising). Some of these chapters will be light-hearted but I could not close the *book without at least a glance at the shadows that are gradually but steadily closing in on the sunny landscape.*

The Sounds of Rome

WHENEVER I AM TRAVELLING IN FARAWAY PLACES THERE are two sounds that always remind me of Rome. The first is the ring of a hammer banging away on a wall of brick or stone, a high-pitched 'tack tack tack' that identifies a stonemason who is mending a brick wall or cutting a tunnel for new electric cables. Rome is the city of masons and for two thousand years men with strong arms have been raising their hammers and whamming them down onto the blunt end of iron chisels to shape the bricks and stones that form the backbone of the Eternal City. I occasionally hear this 'tack tack' on Sundays too, but it is very much milder, when Robert, my sculptor husband, is making bases for his statues out of rough travertine.

The second sound that reminds me of Rome comes in spring and early summer. It is the high, shrill shriek of the swifts returning to Rome from their winter refuge in Africa. After years of watching the skies in spring, Robert and I have discovered that our summer visitors usually reappear on our birthday, 8 April (yes, we have the same birthday), so it has become a custom to celebrate these events by opening a bottle of Prosecco on our Roman terrace as the birds swoop back through the southern skies.

The swiftian flight plan from Africa is always the same. The first few swifts, scouts perhaps, come swirling into the sky high above the Chiesa del Divino Amore (Church of Divine Love) just across the back alley from us. They spin and dive above the church for an hour or so and then, as the sun dips lower, they come closer to catch the insects that fly up from the overheated city. Only then do we finally hear the familiar shriek, which to me is the true sound of the Roman spring.

Although I say that the swifts come back on our birthday I am bound to admit that some years they have kept us waiting for as long as seven days. One year they arrived a full week behind schedule and the papers reported that they had been held up because of unusually heavy sandstorms in Morocco and Algeria. There was also some talk, later denied by bird experts, that their numbers had been decimated by poachers who annually wade into the sea at the tip of Calabria to shoot at birds migrating from Tunis. (The bird people claim that the poachers are really out to shoot eagles and kites, not swifts.)

We decided to throw a terrace party on a recent 8 April to celebrate the swifts' return. It turned out to be a lovely spring afternoon. Our white wisteria was in full flower on the pergola and just below it was our ever-blooming 'Iceberg' rose, which had grown more than a foot in the winter and was displaying at least two dozen ice-white flowers. Pots of white geraniums graced one wall, and a huge silver-grey lavender bush, the biggest I have seen, did the honours next to them. About a dozen guests arrived at sunset armed with binoculars and cameras and we had no sooner assembled on the terrace than a single black swift, slim as a sickle, zoomed through the sky and started tumbling exercises above our heads.

'That's the first scout,' Robert announced as he uncorked a bottle of Prosecco. 'The rest of them should be along soon.' We drank a toast to the scout and then settled down to scan the clouds for the rest of the immigrants. An hour passed and not a single swift appeared. Our friends put away their cameras and began to talk of politics and summer holidays.

Eventually we decided to go out for a pizza as the birds had obviously been delayed. Just as we were heading for the door there was a sudden flurry above us and a great cloud of migrating swifts began tumbling in, fresh from Africa. We could hear them as they came rolling down like curved arrows. And then, as they would do every evening throughout the summer, they joined together in a long roller-coaster fly-past, starting on the west side of the piazza and skimming over the church roof, cutting a big slice beside our apartment before zooming up to the south and west again. At every turn in their circle it seemed as if they might collide with a wall, but they always missed by inches, screaming in chorus as they did so. No Red Arrow formation could be more precise.

We had a final glass of Prosecco as we watched the show before skipping out happily to the local pizzeria, where the waiter asked us what the excitement was all about.

'We're celebrating because the swallows have just come back to Rome,' one guest replied. The waiter shrugged. 'Eh, beh, and so? They come back every year.'

The birds aren't the only delights our terrace gives us. It also serves as our back yard, our garden in the sky, and extends our seasons. While plants in the open country begin to fade in late October, in the city we often have geraniums and roses blooming at Christmas. We get an advance on spring weather as well. If we go to our country house in Canale around Easter, we are always cold. But in the city, spring often steals onto our protected terrace as early as March, and we can feel the heat of the sun while eating lunch. The white wisteria on our Rome terrace flowers three weeks earlier than the lavender-coloured wisteria in the country.

In all our years in Rome we've been very lucky. We have often managed to find small flats for rent with terraces. In some cases the terraces were actually larger than the flats. Our first flat near the Piazza Cavour had only two and a half rooms with a half-bathroom and a half-kitchen, and when we put the rubbish out at night we had to wheel our daughter's cot into the kitchen so that we could open the door. To compensate, our living room gave onto a terrace as big as an ice rink, with a lovely view across Prati to the Castel Sant'Angelo and the great dome of St Peter's. On Saturday nights the Castello would be illuminated like a maharaja's birthday cake and we could almost see angels flying back and forth from the battlements of the ancient fortress to the arched bridge of Ponte Sant'Angelo.

From Prati we moved to a fourth-floor walk-up on the Piazza Scanderbeg near the Fontana di Trevi, which was close enough for Robert to bicycle to his sculpture studio on the Via Margutta every day. This meant a lot of stairs to climb, but it also meant a balcony in the sky wide enough to accommodate a table with three chairs so that at lunchtime we could sit and gaze down at the Quirinale palace and its palm-filled gardens. Jenny, who by then was eight, would always check to see if a blue flag was flying from the palace's turrets, a sign that President Gronchi was in residence.

Sitting at lunch we also had a bird's-eye view of the Eternal City. Looking to the east, we could watch storm clouds gathering above the sea at Ostia. To the north and west, we could see the first snows of winter collecting on the mountain peaks.

Rome seemed like a big cocoon. Nestled low to the ground in its cosy riverine basin with the sea protecting it on one side and the Apennines on the other, the city was contained in a sort of built-in shelter system that few other capitals can claim. No angry tidal waves can come bashing in from the west (the sea at Ostia is a safe fifteen miles away), and to the north and east the city is sheltered from snow and wind by a comforting band of foothills. Even the central river, the Tiber, which used to burst its banks with deadly results every few years, now has high flood-proof walls, so it looks more like a giant underpass than a living body of water.

The bad things that happen in the rest of Italy, like floods and earthquakes and terrible blizzards, never happen in Rome. There are no rumbling volcanoes hovering over it as there are in Naples and Catania, and although the city is listed as lying in the earthquake zone, it has not suffered a major quake since Caesar's time. The Colosseum and the Forum are crumbling, but most of this destruction was caused by Renaissance builders who used the ancient marbles as quarries for new building.

Rome is not only beautiful, it is also intimate and friendly. There are no towering structures of glass and steel to confront you. In fact, aside from St Peter's there are no towering buildings at all. If an old building needs to be repaired, the rule is that the interior can be modernized but the façade must remain exactly as it was created.

Many of the cobbled roads built by the Romans two thousand years ago are still in use. They look attractively quaint and rustic but they are quite unable to handle the crush of modern traffic. Romans now drive thousands of cars and motorcycles through streets that were built for a few hundred horse-drawn chariots, so traffic in the daytime moves slower than a man walking on foot. I have seen a lady in a wheelchair being pushed down the Via Sistina quite a bit faster than the cars were moving. Sooner or later something is bound to give. And when the inevitable gridlock comes, which could be almost any day now, Rome will do what it should have done thirty years ago: it will turn itself back into a walkers' city, with broad pavements and parks.

Among the splendid cities of the world I suspect that Rome has been the most loved by the most people for the longest time. According to Virgil's *Aeneid*, Aeneas ended up in Rome after the fall of his native Troy and a series of romantic adventures in Carthage. His descendants were said to have founded the civilization that became the Roman Empire, although Virgil makes no attempt to explain what connection, if any, existed between his mythical Aeneas, the founder, and the equally mythical founding brothers, Romulus and Remus.

Then came Hannibal, probably the greatest military genius of ancient times, who spent much of his career

trying to conquer Rome. Another famous personality from northern Africa, Queen Cleopatra of Egypt, had a not-so-secret yen for Rome and Romans too. First she had a love affair with Julius Caesar and travelled to Rome with him, sailing up the Tiber in triumph, an event that has been duplicated in glorious Technicolor by Elizabeth Taylor. When Caesar was assassinated she returned to Egypt but wasted no time in becoming the ally and mistress of Caesar's deputy, Mark Antony. Their alliance was highly unpopular with the Romans and especially with Caesar's adopted son, Octavian, who saw their union as a threat to his political ambitions. He declared war on both Antony and Cleopatra and their forces were defeated in the battle of Actium in 31 BC. After this defeat Mark Antony committed suicide; Cleopatra attempted without success to seduce Octavian but when her charms failed she ended her life by submitting to the bite of an asp.

Two of the great saints of Christianity, St Peter and St Paul, travelled as missionaries from the Holy Land all the way to Rome, and both were rewarded for their pains by being tried and then put to death by the tyrant Nero. The remains of St Peter are reported to have been buried under the spot where St Peter's Basilica, the largest of all Christian churches, was later constructed.

All through the Middle Ages and the Renaissance, travellers kept flocking to Rome, although most did not suffer the dreadful fate that befell so many of the early Christians. Velasquez came to paint Roman popes and princes, as did El Greco, and Corot made many drawings of the classical countryside.

Napoleon occupied Rome on 2 February 1808 and set up his brother as King of Naples. His sister, the exquisite Paolina, married into one of the noble Roman families, the Borgheses, and lived in luxury in the Palazzo Borghese (across the street from where we now live). She was reportedly a woman of such divine proportions that the sculptor Canova carved her in marble as a topless Venus. When a shocked friend asked her how she could bear to pose naked for the great artist, the lady replied that it was no trouble as the studio was heated.

Others who came to see Rome and stayed on were the poets Keats and Shelley. Goethe was one of the most appreciative of the German intellectuals who sought the comfort of the Italian sun, and after him the writers came by the dozen: Henry James, Mark Twain, Edith Wharton, Thomas Mann, Ernest Hemingway, Sinclair Lewis and Tennessee Williams. And they all loved Rome.

The one man who seemed strangely unwilling to appreciate Rome was Sigmund Freud. Biographers tell us that on several occasions when he had been planning a trip to Rome from his home in Vienna (which was, after all, an easy train journey), Freud suddenly cancelled his plans without giving an explanation. No one appears to have a clue about his odd reluctance.

Was he ill? Was he suffering from a phobia of travelling? Was he concerned because he had no colleagues to meet in Rome, and no disciples there working on his theories? Or did he fear that his discovery, the talking cure for mental illness, would not go down well with the Italians, who talked a lot anyway, not for therapeutic reasons but just to make a good show or to amuse their relatives? Since he was accustomed to working with patients from northern climes – Germans, Austrians, English and Americans, who were known to be introverted or repressed, full of anxiety and sexual hang-ups – did he perhaps fear that he might be extraneous in Rome? What could a man who specialized in the agonies of the human sub-conscious have to offer to a people who seemed at all times confident, extrovert and without complexes?

The Romans themselves are among the most en-thusiastic Rome-boosters. Take, for instance, the taxi-driver who picked us up at the airport on our return from a holiday in London where it had rained every day. We remarked on how pleasant it was to see the sun again.

He turned around in his seat to face us. 'But naturally,' he said, 'Rome is the place to be. The old Romans weren't so stupid. They ruled the world. They could have moved to a new capital, to Egypt, to London, even to Paris if they wanted. But they chose to stay here.'

As for the citizens of Rome, they strike the visitor as well disposed towards strangers, but behind the smiles there is a certain stand-offishness. They may offer you a coffee at a stand-up bar but they are not likely to invite you to their homes, and even if you go to their address it will be difficult to find them as they are reluctant to put their names on the downstairs buzzers.

The same passion for anonymity applies to their telephone behaviour. Many Romans keep their telephone numbers unlisted. Gas meter readers have a terrible time trying to get into private homes. Census-takers have a similar problem as no Roman is at all anxious to reveal to a stranger the details of his parentage or of his daily life, not to mention the most sacred of all his secrets, his annual income.

Contradictions haunt Roman behaviour. They follow the latest fashions but they also cling to ancient prejudices. There was a time, back in the booming Eighties, when black topcoats were in style and everyone went around looking like funeral directors. The next year it was wall-to-wall green loden. Since the Jubilee year ladies wear short blouses or jackets over very tight trousers and spike heels that get stuck in the cobblestones. Comfort doesn't count.

But, as I have noted, Romans can be very traditional. They avoid chill draughts, and are convinced that moving air-currents bring pneumonia. Because they were brought up as Catholics, they expect to be married in church, with the bride wearing a wedding dress that costs as much as an Alfa Romeo. Yet on Sundays the churches are frequently empty, the priests often from Poland or Hungary, and Italy has the lowest birthrate in Europe and one of the highest levels of abortion.

Romans are anti-government to the core, and fight any official attempts to infringe upon their personal realm or their wallets. But if they can use a VIP connection and get a 'recommendation' for a place in a government bureaucracy where they will have friendly hours, six-weeks' holiday and gilt-edged pensions, they forget their anti-government qualms and climb over their best friends to get the position.

In common with the Spanish and French, the Italians also like to take their holidays at the same time every year, during the months of July and August. Thus every year without fail all the major highways of Italy have twenty- or thirty-kilometre queues waiting at the autostrada toll booths on the first and last weekends of July, and again on the first and last weekends of August. Nothing moves on the Autostrada del Sole going north or south for hours and hours. Helicopters fly overhead gleefully reporting the worst traffic jams of the year and the enraged drivers shake their fists and make gestures to heaven, swearing that they will never take a holiday at this season again. But the following year, traffic queues are longer than ever.

One reason for this is that most Italians don't mind crowding. They are not a solitary people. The vision of an Italian male or female walking on a lonely stretch of the shore is rare indeed; they like to crowd ribcage to ribcage on beaches, and if this is not close enough, buttock to buttock. Despite that reluctance to divulge personal information, there is no word in Italian for 'privacy'.

They have traditional eating habits too. When they order food in their neighbourhood trattoria they try to deal directly with the cook, spelling out exactly how many minutes to cook the risotto or the spaghetti, and how long the meat should be grilled. They specify exactly which greens should be included in the green salad.

They are even more careful about their health; in fact no country on earth can count more hypochondriacs than Italy. Audiences for the three different health programmes on TV are counted in the millions. When mad cow disease struck, Italian beef consumption dropped by 80 per cent in only a few days. When the Chernobyl reactor blew its top in Russia, no one in Rome would eat lettuce for several months. So far not a single case of anthrax has been reported in Italy, but first-aid clinics in Rome claim that they now have to deal with a handful of cases of 'suspected anthrax' every month.

For all this, Rome has been home to us for over forty years. It is to Rome that I owe the inspiration for all that follows.

CHAPTER TWO

Moving Day for the Cook Family

IT WAS MOVING DAY FOR THE COOKS. WE WERE IN THE process of abandoning our old digs near the Fontana di Trevi for a larger flat we'd found in a sixteenth-century palazzo on the Piazza Borghese. It was to be our first flat with a proper terrace.

Jenny, aged eight, and our new *tuttofare* (do-everything maid), Gina, had driven over in the removal van to unload our supply of books, pans and furniture. Robert would be coming soon in our Morris Minor which was filled with statues wrapped in blankets, the family silver and a few big lemon trees that our movers had refused to lug. Since there seemed to be no place for me or my one-year-old son, Henry, in either truck or car, I had decided to wheel him over in his pushchair, stopping on the way to throw a coin into the Trevi Fountain for luck.

We had just reached the front gate of Piazza Borghese 91, our new home, when Jenny rushed down from the third floor to greet us.

'You'd better hurry,' she said. 'The movers are screaming at Gina. They say they're going to just dump everything in the front hall and go away. Gina is yelling at them that she'll call the Carabinieri and send them off to jail.'

I knew Jenny was not exaggerating, for Gina, a portly Roman lady in her mid-forties with a mind of her own, had a mercurial temperament, and the ability to switch from one humour to another with amazing alacrity. Once she got started her voice increased in volume and intensity with every second, and even though I was standing on the first floor I could hear her bellowing at the men on the third. Several tenants in the building had opened their doors a crack so they could hear better.

'Our front door is big enough,' I protested to Jenny. 'All they have to do is open the other half and they can get everything in.'

'It's not *that* door,' Jenny explained. 'It's the little

one that goes from the big entrance into the corridor. The first door is big enough but the second one isn't. The sofa is stuck in the middle.'

I seized Henry and we hurried up the steps to the third floor.

The scene in our new flat was right out of the Marx Brothers. The two big entrance doors had been flung open and all the furniture had been brought into the front hall: two sofas, one *armadio* or wardrobe, a large dining table and eight chairs, and a gargantuan American refrigerator that we had bought second-hand from someone at the US Embassy who had been ordered to Africa (where perhaps he thought fridges grew on trees).

Our smallish yellow sofa had been turned on its end and the two very large removal men, Enzo and his brother Filiberto, were trying to ease it sideways through the narrow door. Then they tried to jam it through head first. But the door into the main part of the flat was much too small. The sofa would not budge.

Gina had placed herself directly behind the two men to prevent them giving up.

'If you can't get it through, *cretini*,' she bellowed, 'you can at least take the door off its hinges and try again.'

Enzo and Filiberto glared. They did not like being called cretins. But they were both from Trastevere, and young men from Trastevere were used to women like Gina. Their mothers, their aunts and most of their neighbours looked and acted like Gina. They might even end up – may the saints protect them – marrying women like Gina.

'But, signora,' they groaned, 'even with the door off the *divano* won't go through. And speaking with respect – *parlando con rispetto* – the *divano* is a heap of junk anyway.'

They pronounced the word 'signora' with a faint sarcasm. Actually, Gina also referred to herself as signora, despite the fact that she had never been married. Her reasoning was that the title gave her added clout in her dealings with sneaky tradesmen, bribeable public-health authorities, tax officials, and all the evil bureaucrats in the Italian pension system.

I tried to introduce a note of calm. 'Why don't you just give it a try, fellows? The door comes off its hinges very easily.' It was my turn for a baleful look from the two brothers. Both of them cast their large and lustrous eyes upon me.

'But, signora,' they whispered, 'the door is too small. We need at least an extra ten centimetres to get that blasted thing through.'

'Why not try?' I whispered back.

Taking deep breaths, they dropped the sofa and removed the door from its hinges. Then they confronted the doorless space with the sofa again.

I turned away to avoid more baleful looks just in time to spot a large tree coming through the front door. It was Robert staggering in with the first of the controversial lemon trees.

Gina rushed to help him. 'Signor Roberto, these *farabutti* [rascals] don't even know how to move a sofa through a door.'

Robert, who had maintained a surprising calm throughout the packing and moving, surveyed the situation at the door and nodded to Enzo. 'You're right,' he said, 'the sofa will never go through. Let's just throw it out.'

'But, Robert, it's beautiful. I made the yellow cover myself.'

'The only way to get it in is to saw off the legs,' Robert concluded.

He put this idea to the men, and without further delay Enzo went to his tool kit and pulled out a rusty handsaw.

Five minutes later, the sofa had been shorn of its wooden legs, dragged unceremoniously the length of the corridor and dumped in the living room.

Robert looked at it squatting solidly on the floor. 'We could always saw the legs off the coffee table too, light incense and play mah-jong.'

How could a Renaissance building have such a narrow doorway? After all, the rooms were large enough to take a sofa, a big television and an even bigger fridge. The answer is that Renaissance palaces were built in squares or rectangles with an open court-yard in the middle and living quarters clustered around the outside. This shape, which I think of as a square doughnut, is actually a design that goes back to classical times. Tenants would enter these courtyards from a single wide doorway, or *portone*, on the street, which was often wide enough to drive a carriage through. There was a smaller wooden door cut in it, where tradesmen would deliver fresh food such as milk and eggs. During the Renaissance these ground-floor courtyards would often be tiled or cobblestoned and many would also have fountains where people from the neighbourhood would come to wash their clothes.

In the more elegant palazzi such as ours, the first floor was called the *piano nobile*, and here the ceilings were high, the windows large and the fittings were made of walnut. It was only much later that we discovered that our palazzo was much more important than we had originally believed: it was once the home of the famous Cardinal Camillo Borghese, who became pope in 1605 and assumed the title of Paul V (of whom more later).

The upper storeys of our building were divided into smaller units for dependants or relatives. These apartments were accessed by stairways, but to enter them each tenant (and his luggage) had to pass through a narrow door to the corridor beyond. Rooms off this corridor-balcony were large enough to contain a bed or two, some chairs and a table, and perhaps an *armadio* and a small desk.

Toilets in Renaissance palaces like ours, if they existed at all, were banished to the ends of the corridors so a single sewage pipe could serve the whole building. If there wasn't room for them, some sixteenth-century builders would cantilever special toilet-balconies with drainpipes leading down to the street. In our flat we do have an ordinary bathroom with all the modern fittings, but in addition we have a secondary ancient toilet and sink clinging to a tiny balcony off the kitchen. Looking out across the street, we see that several apartments there have small toilet-balconies stuck onto the buildings, one on top of the other like double-decker buses, with no visible means of support.

Primitive or not, the smaller rooms in these Renaissance flats were not all that uncomfortable. They could be heated by wood fires or braziers in cold weather, and since each room had a door opening onto the balcony on one side and a big window on the street side, both could be flung open on stifling summer evenings to let the cooler night air circulate. This system still works like a dream, making air conditioning unnecessary in buildings such as ours.

By great good fortune, our apartment had other features not found in the rest of the building. The last two rooms along the corridor had been joined together by some enterprising tenant so we had a gracious living- and dining-space filled with light from three floor-length windows. The last window in this pretty room had been converted into a door, with two steps leading down to a paved rooftop facing due south. This marvellous rooftop space seemed never to have been used for growing flowers, but it had a brick wall around it. All it needed was a hosepipe and some seedlings to become a terrace.

The views from our south-facing windows were pleasant and very Roman. Directly across the street from us was the pretty Chiesa del Divino Amore with its low sloping roof covered by well-worn pink tiles, and a graceful bell tower adorned with inlaid blue mosaics. Since the church is our closest neighbour, lying only about ten metres away from our third-storey windows, we see everything that happens there. We see the big white cat who sometimes comes to crouch behind the peak of the roof in the hope of catching a pigeon. We also see the church mice who come to

eat the breadcrumbs that our neighbour throws there.

We have a good view of the little terrace beside the church roof, so we can watch the nuns who come regularly to trim and water the flowers in the window boxes. They hang out their own long black tunics to dry, and also the vestments belonging to the priest, including his shirts, tunics and purple socks, bought perhaps at a time when he was hoping to be named cardinal. But in our many years opposite the church roof we have never once seen the priest himself attending to his laundry.

The church may today be called the Chiesa del Divino Amore, but a tablet on the wall tells us that it was first named in 1131 after Santa Cecilia, a Christian martyr who converted to Christianity in the third century and managed to convert her husband Valerian and her brother-in-law too. For her sins the poor lady was locked in her own steamroom to die but by a miracle she survived, and emerged singing from her prison. For this reason, she was named patron saint of music. After this ordeal her enemies tried to behead her, but they didn't make a clean job of it – in the three excruciating days that she lay dying she managed to convert another four hundred Romans to Christianity. She bequeathed her palace home to the church of Santa Cecilia in Trastevere. Our small neighbourhood Chiesa del Divino Amore was also dedicated to her because it was believed that it stood on the exact spot where Cecilia's parents had once lived.

But how did the patron saint of mattress-workers

and junk-dealers, San Biagio, contrive to become the second protector of the little church in 1525? It was partly a matter of geography. In the Middle Ages, our district near Piazza Borghese was known as Puzerato (*puzzo* means 'bad smell'), because it was very close to the Tiber River, which was used as a refuse dump and sewer. Records show that the ghetto and city prison were located on the banks of the Tiber too, along with many of the more odoriferous enterprises, such as slaughterhouses and tanning factories.

The mattress-cleaners also settled in our area, poor workers who travelled around the city bearing on their shoulders carding tools bristling with sharp nails. Their job was to collect soiled and lumpy wool mattresses, many of them no longer sweet-smelling, and clean them and card their wool to render them fresh and fluffy again. The mattress men, who still ply their trade in some sections of the city, used to complain that their business was a grubby one. As one unhappy wandering mattress-maker complained in 1589:

> *Io materasse fo l'anno un migliaro*
> *Ne pur in borsa mi trovo un dinaro.*

This translates very freely as:

> I card a thousand mattresses a year at best
> And yet my purse is empty as a raven's nest.

To appease these unhappy fellows, in 1575 the elders of Santa Cecilia's church decided to dedicate it to the

Brotherhood of Mattress-makers and to name it after the martyr and mattress-maker San Biagio. He had been murdered by being ripped to pieces with a carding stick. Some of the more traditional elders complained that it would be unfair to eliminate Cecilia and in the end it was decided to make the two martyrs, Cecilia and Biagio, joint protectors of the church.

Despite the lack of a historical connection between these two, Michelangelo, a man not overly worried about small details, when painting his final fresco, 'The Last Judgement' in the Sistine Chapel, showed San Biagio with his clothes torn off, being rent asunder by his enemies while looking down at an unclothed Santa Cecilia, stretched out on a wheel before her messy beheading. Pope Paul III was horrified when he saw these two saints bare as babes on the wall of the holy Sistina, and in the end Michelangelo was ordered to scrape away some of the plaster so that poor Cecilia could be covered with a rough gown, while Biagio had his head turned the other way so that he could not see, even if he felt so inclined, her dishevelled figure.

Since this time the church has undergone numerous transformations, but in 1802 it was taken over by the brotherhood of the Madonna del Divino Amore, which maintains it to this day. Until recently, when a disco joint and a chic Venetian restaurant with a noisy kitchen moved in to break the calm, our back alley remained a model of decorum, interrupted only about once a month by a madman who comes by soon after midnight and throws stones at the church, bellowing,

'*Gesuiti falsi!*' We have no idea why he is so angry with the Jesuits or why he associates our little church with the Jesuit order.

CHAPTER THREE

Settling In

OUR HOUSEKEEPER GINA HAD BEEN WORKING FOR US FOR only six months when we moved into Piazza Borghese in the spring of 1960, but she had already become a most important member of our family. I still remember the first time she climbed the stairs for interview, when we still lived in our old flat at Piazza Scanderbeg.

A sturdy personage in her mid-forties, she was just under five feet tall and weighed well over a hundred kilos. She carried her weight out in front, creating an off-balance look. Since she was breathing hard after the five-floor climb I asked her to sit down. She let herself down carefully onto a sturdy wooden chair and planted her feet wide apart to aid stability.

She was wearing one of those flowered dresses of dark blue and burgundy, the kind that button up the front and have many pockets. You find them in Italian country markets, and in England they used to sell them as 'house dresses'. Some Italian country ladies wear them year in and year out, taking them off only when they get dressed up to go to a funeral or a wedding. If it is a wedding, they wear the good dress until the ceremony is over and then change into a work dress to help in the kitchen.

As accessories Gina had a very large black bag that might well have started life as a crocodile, and a pair of brand new and rather tight black shoes, which she wore only when she was going out shopping. I was aware, although I never mentioned it in the years I knew her, that she was also wearing new black rayon-acetate underwear, including a black custom-made corset, black bloomers and a petticoat edged with factory lace. All this finery was in case she was hit by a truck driver on the Via del Corso and had to be taken to hospital, where torn or tatty underwear would have disgraced her for ever.

I had heard about the underwear from her older sister, who wore it too. She was a formidable woman named Euleuteria, who had preceded Gina as an occasional babysitter. In fact it was Euleuteria who had suggested that Gina might like to come to us as a housekeeper once we moved to Piazza Borghese.

She explained to me that as the youngest daughter in a family of eight brothers and sisters who grew up in Frascati, just south of Rome, Gina had been singled out as the daughter who would stay at home to take care of her parents when they grew old. This was a not uncommon arrangement in large country families in the south, and Gina had assumed this extra responsibility with good grace. During the war she had helped augment the family income by running a black-market butter and egg business, carrying farm products from the country to sell to rich Romans. But once her parents were dead she did not feel obliged to carry on as family slave for ever. One brother, a prosperous baker, seemed to expect her to come out to his shop in Albano every Friday and Saturday, to help him make extra *maritozzi* (sweet buns) and *ciambelle* (doughnuts) for the weekend markets. During the week Gina found that her numerous nephews and nieces expected her to report to them regularly to help with cleaning, laundering, cooking and babysitting, all without pay.

Both Euleuteria and Gina decided that this kind of family dependence should be discouraged. Rather than working for her relatives, she would be better off in a job with a family where she would be adequately paid and that would also give her a good excuse for not working elsewhere.

I was drawn to Gina from the first because of a certain rebellious sparkle in her eyes. I could just picture her rolling into wartime Rome in an old country bus, carrying under her arm a black marketeer's cardboard suitcase full of butter and eggs, along with some chunks of *caciotto* cheese and tins of dark green olive oil.

The two of us hadn't been talking for more than ten minutes when it was decided that she would start work immediately. I explained that her duties would be to keep the house clean, make the beds every morning, do the family shopping and cook family meals. She volunteered that if she had any time left over in the afternoon, she would enjoy taking one-year-old Henry in his pushchair to the spacious gardens surrounding the Castel Sant'Angelo across the river.

In the next couple of days I got a preview of Gina's abilities. She was the best spaghetti cook around and her spaghetti alla carbonara (a *carbonaio* is a man who makes charcoal) was a complete triumph. First, she would cook the spaghetti and fry up some bacon. The bacon went into a bowl with several lightly beaten raw eggs, then she would add the steaming spaghetti, mix it well and garnish it with sharp pecorino cheese, and lunch was on. The dish is favoured by charcoal-burners who work in the forests making charcoal by burning wood. All these workers need is a handful of spaghetti, a hunk of bacon and a couple of eggs and they're in business.

Gina used a frying pan, or *padella*, for everything else in the kitchen. She fried pork, beef, chickens, aubergine, artichokes and fish. If we were having leafy greens like spinach or Swiss chard, she would first boil these until they were limp and then toss them into the *padella* to fry with garlic and olive oil. Many Roman restaurants still prepare vegetables in this way. All this emphasis on the top of the stove was because Gina's family had never owned an oven.

Her cleaning abilities were limited because she could not bend over or reach up very far. She could not stretch high enough to clean mirrors or pictures or high windows, and she could get down to the floor only by using a mop. But, like many Italian women, she believed that a clean floor is the equivalent of a clean house. So she shuffled around on a flannel cloth that was supposed to pick up floor dust, and also expended hours of her time pushing a square piece of cotton, called a *straccio* or rag, around the floor with a sawn-off broom, or *pala*, from which the bristles had been removed.

She was also an expert bed-maker and beat the sheets and blankets vigorously on the window sill every morning. When she put them back on the bed, she tucked them in so hard it was difficult to get into the bed at all and turning over became a problem. She was an excellent ironer too, which is perhaps not surprising because she put a hundred kilos of solid muscle into the job so that everything she attacked, from sheets to sweaters, from underpants to frilly blouses, came out flatter than a flounder.

But Gina's greatest and most unexpected triumph was in external relations. She appointed herself as our principal gate-keeper, shopping specialist and general ambassador to the outside world. To make sure that other people treated us with the proper respect, she conferred upon Robert the title of Il Maestro, and I became La Dottoressa. Even Jenny at eight was La Signorina. And as I have already noted, on formal occasions she referred to herself as La Signora.

Sociologists from Italy to Britain like to classify Italian society as floating between the two opposing poles of *familismo*, family-centred behaviour, and *clientelismo*, a system where people get ahead by dint of recommendations from important people. *Familismo*, sometimes known as *familismo amorale*, is a system whereby members of a well-knit family join together in an *azienda familiare* or family firm such as a grocery shop or a restaurant (with mamma at the cash register) or even a small hotel, where the family members form a kind of armed guard to keep out census-takers and other suspicious persons. These family enterprises sometimes grow very large in Italy, which results in family trusts such as those of the Berlusconis, the Agnellis and the Benettons.

I suspect that in a world organized in this way, Gina, by appointing herself our protectress, gave us a slant that we might otherwise have missed on how to survive in Italy. Unconsciously she transferred to us much of the affection and support that she had originally given to her own family; over the years she took care of us when we were sick, procured medicines in highly mysterious ways and kept a stern watch over any *operaio* (worker) who came to repair the flat, making sure that he was never left alone in any room, especially near the family silver. She also made friends with the neighbour who had a small terrace adjoining ours, Maresciallo Palinetti, who worked for the criminal division of the Questura. She would spend a lot of time telling the Maresciallo how most Americans were not as rich as people thought they were. When we received, one black day, a post-card summoning us to an obscure office to report at once 'about a matter of *contributi*' (contributions), which could have concerned fees for collecting rubbish, she gave the report to the Maresciallo and we never heard of the matter again. Papers disappearing from official desks are a constant problem in Italy.

Once we had got the legs nailed back onto our yellow sofa, we began, with Gina's help, to make the apartment habitable. To tell the truth, it was not in any way equipped for modern living. In America and Britain, it is common for a rented apartment, even an unfurnished one, to come with most of the amenities in place. 'Everything but the kitchen sink' is our expression for a great quantity of possessions. But in Italy this whole concept of abundance is turned inside out, because the only thing you will find in a newly rented Roman kitchen is the kitchen sink. There is no stove, no fridge, no hot-water system, and naturally no iron and no vacuum cleaner. And in the whole room there is only one wall plug for all appliances.

When we moved in, the bathroom had only the most basic fittings: bath, toilet, sink and bidet. 'Any stuff that is cemented down or screwed in, so they can't remove it,' was how Robert put it. But even in the bathroom, as in the kitchen, there were dismal clumps of bare electrical wires, so we had to go out and buy every light fixture in the flat. If we wanted more than one light socket in a room we had to call in an electrician. Occasionally we got confused between the two systems, 220 plugs for industrial current and 120 for light fixtures, and ended up burning out can-openers and egg-beaters.

Still another problem was that, only a few months before we found our apartment, the architect of the Catholic Insurance Company of Verona (our landlord, whom we always referred to as La Cattolica) had put the building through a major renovation. The architect dug out the lovely old *cotto* (cooked) tiles that look like polished leather and replaced them with *terrazzo* tiles that resembled slices of brick-coloured mortadella. He also ripped out some of the venerable chestnut beams in the ceilings, and those that he couldn't rip out for structural reasons he plastered

over with industrial-style white stucco. *Orrendo*!
While he was at it, he covered the walls with a brown-
flecked wallpaper, the kind that you find in dentists'
waiting rooms.

Gina turned out to be a great asset in all depart-
ments. She was good at changing plugs and she also
offered to put a magnet onto our electricity meter (to
slow down the number of kilowatt hours recorded),
but in a fit of civic righteousness we told her to skip
the magnet. When it came to shopping, she excelled.
The market was her natural habitat and she shopped
there with the confidence of Queen Victoria. In her
first week she did a tour of all the fruit and vegetable
stands to determine which vendors were the best. She
discovered a farm-lady from Frascati who grew nearly
all her greens in her own *orto* (vegetable garden), from
the smallest and most tender green beans to the biggest
artichokes. She had all the salad greens in season as
well – *scarola*, which has a smooth leaf, *indivia*,
which is crinkly, and a winter salad with four tiny
leaves that she called *bocca di prete* (priest's mouth).
This turned out to be a variety of *valeriana*, a herb that
provides the natural tranquillizer valerian. Gina was
equally adept in the fruit department: she had a knack
for telling when each fruit was at its peak, and we
never got an apple, pear, apricot, plum, strawberry,
melon or fig that was not perfectly ripe.

To check out the butchers and the cheese vendors
Gina descended to the basement level of the market,
where she found a butcher named Giuseppe. He never
disappointed her when she asked for a *filetto* (fillet of
beef) or a nice tender tongue, which she cooked with a

sweet and sour sauce. (Some Roman cooks we knew
cooked tongue with chocolate.) He could also cut very
thin slivers of beef to be served raw with *rughetta*
(rocket) and slivers of Parmigiano. This excellent dish is
called *carpaccio*. The cheese vendor whom she chose
was a country fellow called Sor (short for 'Signore')
Armando. He had dozens of different cheeses, oils and
seasonings and he served capers from a big bottle, and
salted anchovies preserved in huge ten-pound tins that
still bore labels from canning factories in Naples.

The bread sold in the market did not please Gina; it

was not as fresh as it should be, and since bread was the staff of life to her she wanted the best. She therefore made a tour of all the bakers in the neighbourhood until she found one on the Via della Scrofa that lived up to her standards. This shop was a ten-minute walk from the market, so she made it a habit to buy the bread first, when it was just coming out of the oven. She then returned to our palazzo to leave the bread with the *portiera* while she went to the market.

Bread in Italy comes in many different shapes and sizes, each variety having its own passionate group of fans. The biggest and probably most popular type is the great big family-sized loaf called a *pagnotta* (or *panella* in the south), which looks like a cushion with rounded edges. Each loaf weighs about two kilos. This loaf comes with salt (*con sale*) or without salt (*senza sale*) and people differ on which they prefer, but the variety with salt is said to keep longer. The loaf can be made with tender wheat or hard wheat (*grano duro*) and Gina much preferred the hard kind, partly because it keeps a week if stored in a dark place while the tender-grain loaf starts to get stale within twenty-four hours. The hard-grain loaf also has a harder crust, which many Italians prefer; the tender grain has a spongy texture reminiscent of the soft white breads so popular in Britain and America.

There are other, smaller varieties of bread for all tastes. One of the favourites was a roll the shape of an ear of corn called a *ciriola*. This bread roll was very popular because it was crusty, and government subsidies fixed its price at a low level so that it would be available to even the poorest. Gradually bakers stopped producing the beloved *ciriola* because they could make more money with the unregulated *rosetta*, which was shaped like a big rose but lacked crust.

These rolls were used for afternoon snacks, and when she was growing up in the country, where sweets were expensive, Gina would eat bread with squashed figs or bread with chestnut paste. A common dish for farmers was *pan cotto*, where bread that had gone stale was softened in hot water, and then garnished with a beaten egg. In the south near Naples, where bread was and is perhaps the most common item in the diet, there are some old expressions: *mazzi e panelli fanno figli belli* (spankings and bread make children beautiful), and *panelli senza mazzi fanno figli pazzi* (bread without spankings makes the children crazy).

CHAPTER FOUR

A Terrace Is Born

ONCE WE HAD THE TABLES AND CHAIRS IN PLACE, WE decided to start work on the terrace. It was looking pathetic with only two lemon trees and six pots of pink geraniums sitting in a corner.

'The first thing we have to do,' I told Robert at dinner, 'is to put in a water supply.'

'Water? We've got plenty of water,' Robert said. 'Just bring a bucket of water from the kitchen.'

I had had experience of makeshift watering arrangements in earlier apartments and I knew all about broken hoses and water getting spilt on parquet floors.

'If I have to hand-carry water from the kitchen down the hall, across the living room and down the three steps to the terrace, I'd rather not have a terrace at all,' I said.

Gina didn't help much by assuring us it would be no trouble at all to lug a few buckets of water from the kitchen to the terrace every morning. But I was determined; if I was to do any serious terrace gardening in Rome, I would need a proper, piped supply of water. I bided my time until I was certain Robert would be out all day at the bronze foundry. Then I called in a local plumber, Signor Cademartori, who had a small shop on the Via della Lupa just down the street from us. He came wearing a white jacket and studied our piping system with all the concentration of a heart surgeon.

First he looked over the pipes in the kitchen, shaking his head and muttering '*medievale*' to himself. Then he proceeded to the bathroom where he seemed to find the pipes a bit more to his liking. Eventually he located a water pipe that carried water into the cistern above the toilet, and then switched his attention to the window next to the pipe.

'What I must do is carry a special water pipe from the cistern out along the building to the street,' he explained.

Then he went down to the street where the Via della Lupa joined the Vicolo di San Biagio, and studied how to get the pipe around the corner. Eventually he returned to the terrace where Gina and I were just starting to rearrange the pots.

'I think I have the solution,' the learned man said. 'I can do it but it won't be easy. And it won't be cheap.' This last sentence alerted Gina.

'*Quanto*?'

The plumber turned to look at her with surprise. He was not accustomed to a challenge from housekeepers.

'Well,' he said, raising his voice, 'we will have to build scaffolding from the street to the pipe at that corner, and then bring it around to your terrace. There is a gap of twenty metres, and since I cannot fly I cannot secure the pipe to the wall without scaffolding.'

'How much?' Gina insisted.

'Well,' he said softly, 'the scaffolding will cost at least half a million, and then there is my time too. It will take several days . . .'

'So?'

'So it would cost you only one million lire.'

'One million lire!' Gina trumpeted, throwing her glance heavenward.

After some more consultation we sent the plumber away, telling him (falsely) that we would call him back.

'There is only one thing to do,' Gina said with determination. 'We must get my nephew Piero, *subito*!'

'Piero?' I asked.

'He has climbed the Dolomites, so he has a big rope he can tie to the top of the building. Then he can come down the side of the building like a bird.'

She told me how her brother Fabrizio, a baker in Albano, had been unable to erect an antenna for his new television set because his *antennista* (antenna man) complained that the roof was too high and too steep, and he was afraid of falling. Piero was called, and in a short time he had attached an antenna to the chimney, along with all the extra bits and pieces needed to get the big Rome TV stations and the Vatican radio.

As Gina explained to me, Piero was an anomaly in Roman family life. He was a downwardly mobile young man. Piero's father, Aldo, was considered the most successful of Gina's family, and had made the historic shift from a small town in the country to life in the big city of Rome in one heroic leap. He had studied bookkeeping and then surprised everybody by

securing a position at the headquarters of the Roman
gas company on the Piazza Barberini. In the process he
transformed himself from a homespun country boy on
a motorcycle to a city slicker in a tailor-made suit who
drove to work in his own Alfa Romeo.

But there is a certain irony in Aldo's triumph. By
moving his family away from the narrow life of the
small town, he had exposed Piero to new and radical
ideas that rarely filtered through to a country village.
Piero was stimulated by the atmosphere in the Rome
liceo (senior school) and soon joined the school
debating society, where he established himself as an
exponent of left-wing ideology. He also became a top
athlete, his favourite sports being water polo and
soccer. During the holidays he joined a group who
bussed off to the Dolomites to take courses in rock-
climbing. Aldo and his wife watched their son's
development with some vexation: they had brought
their children to the big city hoping to improve their
economic condition, but it had never occurred to them
that their brightest son would dream of turning his
back on the middle-class lifestyle that they had so
recently acquired. Gina reported to me that Aldo's
biggest disappointment had been when he arranged
for Piero to be interviewed by the chief bookkeeper at
the gas company and Piero refused to go.

' "I am not going to put on a suit and work in an
office where I have to kowtow to all the bosses," ' Gina
told me, imitating Piero's response in a high falsetto.
' "I would rather rob a bank than take up a position as
a government slave." ' I could tell that secretly she was
applauding her rebellious nephew.

Piero made a considerable impression when he presented himself at Piazza Borghese the next morning. He was a tall, sturdy young man with piercing eyes and curly jet-black hair cut in an Afro style, and by dint of much scuba-diving and mountain-climbing he had been able to avoid the family tendency to put on weight. He surveyed the pipe and terrace situation, carefully measuring distances and taking down notes in a small notebook, and the next day he came back with a skinny friend called Eugenio, who he said was an apprentice plumber. The two of them were carrying several sections of piping and a black bag full of tools and pipe joints. The next thing I knew, Piero was slowly descending from the roof on a kind of rope chair that Eugenio had secured from above. The view of Gina's nephew dangling in the air three full storeys above the street made me dizzy, so I closed my eyes, but when I opened them I could see that he was securing the water pipe to the east side of the building. Then he made a joint with a special right-angle fixture, and before long he was bobbing alongside the south wall of the building until he was above our terrace. From there he had nothing to do but send a pipe down to the terrace level and attach a tap. A triumph all round. At Gina's suggestion, I gave each of our new plumbers 100,000 lire, and they appeared happy. When Robert came home from the foundry that evening, he found me out on the terrace hosing down the dusty lemon trees.

It took me several months to discover that just because someone is good at outdoor gardens it doesn't necessarily follow that he will be a great terrace gardener too, because plants don't grow the same way in pots as they do in open gardens. Plants in pots are delicate. You can't simply plant up your pots on a nice spring morning and assume that the sun and the rain will take care of them for the rest of the week; for while a garden planted in the soil tends to get better all the time, a garden in pots goes downhill unless it is given lots of special care.

In an open garden, leaves, clippings and cut-off rosebuds, and sometimes apple cores and old figs, are constantly dropping onto the soil. They add compost and friability so that it becomes light and hospitable, and attractive to earthworms.

The common earthworm is of vital importance in maintaining soil fertility. It aerates and pulverizes the soil. It actually produces topsoil. Without its aid soils would be relatively hard-packed. The earthworm is nature's plough. It bores into the soil and keeps it well aerated, a condition which encourages soil microbes to multiply. Such tunnelled earth permits water to penetrate rather than run off and to maintain the moist condition so necessary to plant life.

The authority behind these words is none other than the great father of evolution, Charles Darwin, the naturalist, who in 1881 published a little-known volume entitled *Vegetable Mould and Earthworms*. Darwin wrote his book only after years of tireless investigation into the part earthworms play in nature's scheme of things, concluding that without the earthworm vegetation would struggle to survive.

According to Darwin, in making their burrows worms swallow an enormous quantity of earth, out of which they extract any digestible matter it may contain, such as fresh and half-decayed leaves and other organic materials. They work mostly in the top layer of soil, aerating it and allowing oxygen to penetrate to the roots of plants. Without this oxygen, the plants could not grow.

I have often wondered whether you can trust earthworms not to eat plants growing in pots. I used to worry that perhaps the worms *pretended* to be aerating the soil, but were really picnicking on the roots of my favourite amaryllis bulbs. But Jenny, who has grown into an expert on compost gardening, says that my fears are unwarranted; that worms are basically in business to consume rotting plant material and almost never make a meal of healthy roots or bulbs. Or, as Darwin put it:

> Where the farmer or gardener permits the soil to become so sterile of organic matter that the earthworm in desperation turns to the roots for sustenance, there will arise also other more evil consequences. On the other hand, where there is sufficient humus in the soil, root growth will become very vigorous and the number of fine root hairs will far outnumber those on plants growing in soil that contains less organic matter.

But beware! Although earthworms are good for potted plants, the same does not apply to other small creatures such as slugs, grubs and beetles and their larvae, which chew up everything they can find in pots, especially growing roots.

There is still another category of organism, even smaller than slugs or beetles, which contributes mightily to the health of soils. These organisms are known as 'soil bacteria', and the garden dictionary describes them as 'the chief agents in bringing about putrefaction and decay in the soil and thus ... most important in the production of humus'. The dictionary adds that some of the bacteria concentrate on taking nitrogen from the air and fixing it in the soil. (This process occurs, for instance, when you introduce nitrogen-rich plants such as clover or alfalfa, whose roots transmit nitrogen and other necessary vitamins to the compost.) Some agronomists are so keen on these bacteria and their magic powers that they have written whole books on them. But for my purposes, it is enough to know that the compost you put into pots should be of high quality, with a gritty or crumbly feel to it like broken-up digestive biscuits.

I used to bring some bags of earth from my compost pile in the country to my friend Eugene Walter, who had one of the best terrace gardens in Rome. The compost reminded him of 'crumbling fudge – it looked so good I wanted to eat it', he said. 'And don't forget,' he would add, 'that every single time you water a plant, the water that comes out of the bottom of the pot is entirely different from the water you put in.' In other words, every time a plant is watered some of the fine vitamins and minerals that are essential to plant health come flooding out of the hole in the bottom.

Your watering is gradually leaching away much of the goodness in the soil, and eventually this will make the plant weaker.

All this tells me that plants in pots need a lot of help from their friends. They need extra water, far more water than you would give them if they were in the earth, and quite a bit of artificial food to boot. In fact I have found that those of my gardening friends who have super terraces buy the best plant food on the market, and this makes their plants young and old flourish.

Another question that is raised repeatedly in gardening circles is what kind of pots are best on a terrace? Should they be plastic or terracotta? And do you have to put broken pots or rubble in the bottom to ensure drainage?

I am well aware that Christopher Lloyd, creator of the famous garden at Great Dixter, insists on crockery pots, and so did Vita Sackville-West. I agree with them that hand-made terracotta pots from Tuscany can be works of considerable charm, especially if they are decorated with the classic designs of the Renaissance or are formed like old Roman oil jugs. But, in an age when muscular garden helpers are thin on the ground, I cling stubbornly to plastic pots. My argument is based on practicality. Plastic pots, tinted a pleasant terracotta, cost much less, probably a tenth of what a good terracotta one will cost, and they don't break, which is another saving. This unbreakability is becoming every day more important, for many of the larger garden-supply firms are no longer offering terracotta at all as it is too heavy and breakable to be transported economically.

For me, the most important asset of plastic pots is that they are movable. In many flowering borders mobility is limited. In a terrace with plastic pots, you can simply whisk unattractive plants out of sight and bring forward others at the precise moment they are in flower. This is very easy to do with bulbs such as tulips or crinums in the spring, and agapanthus and dahlias in midsummer. When they have finished blooming they can be banished to the back row again.

This does not mean that you have to play musical chairs with your terrace plants all year. I try to establish some big pots full of plants that look nice most of the year, like lavender and Leptospermum and even some of the long-season roses, such as the glorious white 'Iceberg' that in Rome blooms gallantly in December. I place these strategically in spots that will catch the eye and I move the other seasonal plants around them.

I have discovered several bulbs that grow much better for me in pots than they do in the ground. One of my favourite summer flowers, the agapanthus, is a case in point. Each time I planted bulbs in the border they seemed to settle in happily and their leaves made a reassuring clump every summer, but when blooming

time arrived there were only one or two flowers. Eventually I dug up half of one patch and replanted the twenty bulbs in four largish pots on the terrace, where they were watered and fed regularly. Last July, when I had a spare moment, I counted the number of flowers I was getting from my four big pots, and discovered thirty-four cerulean blooms. I often move one or two of these pots close to the lavender, which also flowers in early summer: the blue of the agapanthus next to the violet of the lavender is the loveliest colour combination you can find in any summer garden.

And now for a final word on pots, or more particularly the bottom of pots. Some time early in my career as a pot gardener, I read a piece in the prestigious *Garden* magazine (of the Royal Horticultural Society) that said it was unnecessary to put broken crockery or pebbles into the bottom of pots for drainage.

The author claimed that no drainage material was needed because water could find its way through the regular potting soil just as easily as it could through pebbles or rocks. He used terms such as 'osmosis' and 'hydrometric' to support his argument, and I was impressed enough to try potting a few plants without any deliberate drainage. It turned out (as I should perhaps have known) that the pots without stones and broken pottery in the bottom became waterlogged in a surprisingly short time. The water just sat on the surface like a small pond, and the plants started to grow slimy. This happened to one flourishing vine of white wisteria, and two lemon trees that were covered with golden fruit. I had no choice but to turn these unfortunate pots on their sides and dig out the earth using a large cleaver and hammer, so that I could repot them with a lot more drainage material. It took me several hours to change the soil for the lemon trees, because I was anxious not to disturb any of the lemons that were gallantly ripening on their branches. One lemon tree came through intact, but the second had to be jostled a great deal and eventually lost three lemons, which I turned into lemon marmalade. Since then I have always put pebbles or broken crockery into my pots.

CHAPTER FIVE

Walking Henry to School

ONCE THE TERRACE WAS ESTABLISHED WE DECIDED THAT IT was time to try to find some useful activity for Henry. By our second winter at Piazza Borghese Henry had turned two, and it seemed to us that he had more energy than anyone else in central Rome. He loved to charge around on the terrace playing soccer with tennis balls, and although it was perfectly safe because we had attached chicken wire to the top of the terrace wall, it was not enough.

Henry needed more outlets. In his room he had a lot of plastic toys that were washable and educational, and blocks painted with a special non-toxic paint. But these toys bored Henry. He wanted to do more exciting things – the things he saw other people doing. When he went into the kitchen and saw Gina cutting up a half-kilo of potatoes, he would climb up onto a chair and say, 'Io, Ito.' And when he saw Robert drilling holes in the walls to hang pictures he would try to take the drill away from him saying 'Io, Ito.'

Actually, like most foreign children born in Rome, Henry seemed more comfortable speaking Italian than

English, because that was the language the other children spoke in the Castel Sant'Angelo park. He therefore thought of himself as 'Enrico', but since his pronunciation was still imperfect he said 'Ito' rather than 'Enrico'. The word 'me' in Italian is 'io'. So when Henry said 'Io, Ito' he was really trying to say 'Me, Henry' or even 'Let Henry do it.'

We knew something had to be done when he picked up a habit of pushing chairs around the flat so that he could climb up onto desks and take things that he shouldn't, like long scissors or Elmer's Glue. Jenny, who was nine and quite grown up, said maybe it was time to take Henry to some kind of day school, and I asked around and found out there was a kindergarten only a few streets from our house, in the Palazzo Taverna.

I went to see the school, and found it located in a sunny wing of the old palazzo, with its own little walled garden – a perfect place for a school. The matron, Signora Laura Bettarelli, explained that the people who had founded the Montessori school system wanted to break away from the formal, highly disciplined educational style that prevailed in most Italian kindergartens, especially those run by Catholic nuns.

'We want our children to learn to play together, and to avoid a system that is centred on keeping the children quiet and out of trouble,' she said.

I explained to her that Henry was an extremely active little boy, who would no doubt benefit from contact with other children of his own age.

'How old is he?' she asked.

When I told her she agreed that two was a bit young. 'They usually come to us at three,' she added, 'but let's have a look at your son. He sounds quite . . . advanced.'

So the next day I brought Henry round to meet her, and the lady accepted him on the spot.

'I think Enrico is absolutely ready for the school,' she said, smiling. I could only say a small prayer that the school would be ready for Henry.

This happy find changed the pattern of our days, as it involved getting Henry to school at nine o'clock in the morning, and fetching him when the noon cannon went off on the Gianicolo. Since it was such a nice walk, I decided to take Henry to and from school myself: that way I could combine shopping with a bit of sight-seeing in the streets around the Pantheon and the Piazza Navona.

Henry's uniform for the school was basic. Since he was starting school in midwinter he had to wear trousers and a warm coat with a wool hat and mittens. He had to carry a picnic basket containing a small apron, a sandwich and a piece of fruit for a mid-morning snack.

Our walk followed nearly the same course each day. On a typical morning we would come out of our building around eight thirty and I would give Henry the money to buy me a *Herald Tribune*. Behind the newsstand was the great triangular hulk of the Palazzo Borghese, which I explained to Henry was often called the 'Clavicembalo' because it was shaped like a harpsichord. Henry wasn't as interested in the name as he was in the dozens of enormous chimneys that

adorned its roof. He couldn't understand why any
building needed so many chimneys, and I explained to
him that in the old days every room had its own fireplace for heating, and each fireplace had its own
chimney. So Henry counted the chimneys again, one
by one, but he got mixed up after eight and I counted
for him, and reached twelve.

From the newspaper stand we turned to the left and
walked down towards the Via Monte Brianzo, which
took us south along the Tiber River. Here Henry
wanted to cross over to walk beside the Tiber, because
the plane-tree leaves were lying thick on the pavement
and he loved to shuffle great clumps of wrinkled
leaves in front of him.

About halfway down, workers from the gas company were digging a trench in the street, and Henry
forgot about the leaves and rushed over to see what
was going on in the hole. He asked two of the

workmen who were digging there what they were looking for, and they said they were looking for gas pipes. Then one of them picked up a big hammer and tapped a large round pipe to show what he meant. But by this time Henry's attention had shifted to a large iron bucket with charcoal burning in it, which had been placed next to the hole. Every once in a while, when the workers' hands and feet got cold, they climbed out of their trench and warmed themselves over the fire. Henry wanted to warm his hands too, but he was afraid of going too close to the burning coal.

Without their leaves the plane trees along the river were bare, and one could see the opposite shore more clearly. Way downriver, on the far shore, I could just make out the cupola of St Peter's peering from the morning mist. I have always felt that there is something Asiatic about St Peter's. It makes me think of the Taj Mahal or the pleasure-dome of Kubla Khan, despite the fact that Michelangelo apparently copied the dome from the Pantheon, which is wide and flattish like a Buddhist stupa.

The Castel Sant'Angelo, just across the river from us, was a much more appealing building to my mind. I liked its gardens and moat where Henry went to play and learned to ride his first tricycle. I also found it an authentic piece of Roman history: it had started as a tomb for the Emperor Hadrian and in the Dark Ages, when barbarians began sacking Rome, it had been converted into a fortress. As the Vatican grew and the papacy came under threat, an elevated walkway was built between St Peter's and the castle, and a number of popes had to be evacuated along the walk to avoid capture. In 1527, Pope Clement VII, a Medici pope, had to scramble along the passage when the building was attacked by a multinational force of Protestants and Catholics; his progress was dangerously slowed because he insisted on wearing bulky court robes complete with a train. In the end he was saved when one of his cardinals picked up the train and hoisted it over his shoulders, dragging His Holiness into the safety of the castle walls just in time.

After we had finished inspecting the gas excavations, Henry and I crossed the street again and headed through the Piazza Zanardelli, where there were a number of artisan shops. One of them was a marble workshop and when the weather was good the workers came outdoors to polish their marble tables and fireplaces on the pavement. They all wore hats made out of folded newspapers to keep the dust out of their hair, but there was still a thin covering of white marble on their faces. Back in Roman times great vessels carrying marble from Greece and Sicily and northern Italy used to dock at the port of Ostia and huge chunks of the stone would be floated down the Tiber on barges and unloaded at exactly the same spot where now, two thousand years later, marble carvers are still chipping away at the lovely white stone.

We next proceeded in the direction of the Via dei Coronari, and took a short cut down a narrow alley full of big Roman cats. Henry loved cats, but he was always a little wary of street cats because they did not seem to like being patted. But there was one big cat named Mafalda who belonged to a milk store, and she never hissed. Signora Minerva, who ran the store, always gave Mafalda a cup of fresh milk, and at lunch she cooked some tripe for her, so Mafalda could afford to sit out in the sun on a fallen Roman column and be pleasant to little boys.

Further along this street was the house where Anna Maria lived. Anna Maria was two and a half years old but she didn't go to school yet, so she stood in her doorway and waved to Henry as he went by. If we were in good time Henry would run over to talk to her, and sometimes he would open his picnic basket to show her what was inside. Her mother often came to greet Henry too, and invite him into the house for some fresh *pizza bianca* (with just oil and garlic) from the bakery.

Leaving Anna Maria, we crossed the big open piazza of San Salvatore in Lauro, 'San Salvatore in the Laurel Trees', so called because a famous grove of laurels once grew on the spot. Then we started up a little path that led from the piazza to a back door of the Palazzo Taverna. Halfway up this hill, a group of workmen were busy mixing cement and sawing old boards in half, apparently preparing to pour a concrete footpath. Naturally Henry couldn't resist the temptation to put down his basket and try to move their wheelbarrow, but it would never budge an inch.

When we opened the outside gate, Henry would set off through the garden, past the lemon and orange trees, to arrive at a door with a bell-chain attached. A teacher came to let Henry in, and he raced into the schoolroom without a backward glance. I let him go without even a goodbye kiss, as I had already been told by the Montessori teachers that parents were not encouraged to enter the classroom. They felt that the presence of watchful parents might hamper the natural exuberance of the children.

Three hours later, when the noon cannon sounded, I went to fetch Henry, who would have much to tell me about the morning's activities. Then he ran down the footpath towards the Piazza San Salvatore, where a group of neighbourhood boys usually played a midday game of soccer. Henry liked to watch for a while, although he realized that he was too young to join in.

We would proceed down the Via dei Coronari until we came to the little church of the Portuguese. Beyond the

church stands an old tower known as the Tower of the Monkey. At the very top there is a shrine where a light burns day and night. Henry often asked me to tell him the story of the monkey.

I would tell him that once upon a time a nobleman lived in this building with his only son and a large pet monkey. One day the monkey picked the little boy up in his arms and carried him to the top of the tower, where he sat chattering and making fun of all the people below. The little boy's father was in despair for fear the monkey would throw his child onto the street, so he vowed that if the monkey brought his boy safely down, he would build a shrine at the top of the tower and keep a light burning there for ever. Soon afterwards the monkey carried the child down to his father, who built the shrine as he had promised.

Saturday was one of Henry's favourite days, because Jenny could accompany us on our walk to Palazzo Taverna. Often when school was over, if we had time, I would take the children to visit Robert in his studio on the Via Margutta, the famous old street of artists. Robert's studio was located in the open courtyard at No. 51A, famous among movie buffs as the place where Gregory Peck's character, an American journalist, lived when he was entertaining the visiting princess Audrey Hepburn in *Roman Holiday*.

The studio, which had been a stable, was full of Robert's statues; some of them were finished pieces in cast bronze while others were still in beeswax, not yet ready to be taken to the foundry. No one was allowed near the waxes, because if they were pushed or pulled even an inch or two out of line, the casts would have to be banged and rewelded to correct their position. There were also modelling stands in the studio, where models often posed. From time to time both Jenny and Henry were called down to pose for their father, who eventually completed a series of bronzes of each child growing up.

Sometimes we would all go to the Piazza Navona. The piazza, I explained to them, was built more than two thousand years ago as a stadium for Roman games. Boxing matches were held there, and in the warmer weather they had horse races. During the Middle Ages, when the popes ruled Rome, they used to flood the square so that the people could use it as a kind of early swimming pool.

Henry and Jenny loved to go to the piazza at Christmas time, when the whole square was turned into an outdoor Christmas fair. They would watch the man who made ribbon candy, in a booth just beside the famous fountain of the rivers. First he boiled his sugar and water in a great copper vat, then he added the colours, and then he pulled the sticky mess out until it made a series of long, thin candy canes. He always gave a cane to both Henry and Jenny.

They also went to the stands where ceramic workers from Naples displayed their crèche figures of the madonna and the *bambino Gesù* and the three kings coming to pay homage. (The fact that the three kings looked like shepherds from the Campania didn't bother anyone.) And speaking of shepherds, real-life shepherds from the mountains of the Abruzzi would come to play Christmas songs such as '*Tu Scendi dalle Stelle*' ('You Come Down from the Stars') on their flutes and bagpipes. These *zamponieri* (pipers) wore woollen trousers with rough homespun capes made of sheep hide and their shoes were cut out of sheep leather, tied around the ankles with long leather laces. The wail of the bagpipes in the chilly streets during the Christmas season is another Rome sound that stays with me always.

The last stop on our way home was the market for old books and maps, which are sold from portable counters in the piazza in front of our building. Henry knew all the booksellers in this market because he passed by two or three times a day. He liked to look especially at the old prints of horses and sailing boats that they pinned up for sale on a rope with wooden clothespegs.

When we got back home Gina would help Henry take off his coat and ask him what he had done that day, and he would tell her that he was making something wonderful for everyone at Christmas. But he couldn't tell anybody what it was.

'*È un segreto, un segreto!*' he said. '*Neanche Babbo Natale non lo sa.* [It's a secret! Even Father Christmas doesn't know.]'

I'll always believe that the city of Rome, with all its history, is the best playground of the imagination for any child to grow up in.

CHAPTER SIX

A Bad Year for Bicycle Thieves

Every terrace gardener needs an errand boy to help with the fetching and carrying, and I am happy to report that Robert has proved to be a winner in this department. When we first started growing plants in pots he used to dash around to nurseries and markets in our old Morris Minor, but as traffic got worse and parking became impossible he had to think up alternative ways of getting around Rome in a hurry.

Being a man of great impatience Robert considered that walking was a waste of time, waiting at a bus stop the undertaking of an idiot and hiring a taxi a sure path to bankruptcy. So he decided to try a bicycle – or, to be more precise, he became aware of an old red bicycle that a friend had left in a corner of his studio when he returned to America. Within a week Robert became the bicycle terror of central Rome and within a month he also became the scourge of half the bicycle thieves of the city.

Robert's progress across Rome on a bicycle was something to instil fear in even the bravest. Like a guided missile he sprinted the wrong way down one-way streets, frightened dog-walkers and zoomed up and down the Tiber on the pavements. Proud of his prowess, he began to time himself with a stopwatch. He soon found, with a certain bitter joy, that he could get from our flat on the Piazza Borghese to our Neighbourhood Council on the Via Giulia in three minutes flat. (These trips were needed to complain about rubbish or property taxes or other municipal transgressions. His record for the round trip, including the filling-in of necessary forms, was seven and a half minutes.) He could get over to the Trionfale Flower Market in exactly five and a half minutes, and he even set up a special carrier on the back of his bike to take potted plants. He could pedal to the Santo Spirito Hospital in four minutes if anyone he knew was lying sick there, but he considered the Salvator Mundi up on the Gianiculum Hill off limits. Robert's bête noire was hills, and particularly the Via Veneto hill where the Internal Revenue Service for the US Embassy was located. Whenever Robert got threatening tax notices from the US government he was fit to be tied. (Usually they wanted something obscure like a receipt to prove that he had paid his income tax back in 1976.)

The problem wasn't so bad when the Revenue Service was hidden away like a fugitive in an unmarked building on the Via Sardegna, because he could lock up his bike at the bottom of the moving staircase in the Piazza di Spagna and ride up to the Via Veneto in six minutes. (He once tried to ride his bike on the moving stairway but the authorities intervened.) But when the office was relocated right inside the consular office at the other end of the Via Veneto he had to pump uphill, heartened only by the knowledge that afterwards he could coast all the way home.

Robert's battle with the bicycle thieves started in a rather modest way but it soon erupted into full-scale war, and there was a time when the thieves were three up on Robert. In the early days he tended to be neglectful. He once left his bike chained to a post in the Piazza Borghese for nine full days and no one bothered it. That led to overconfidence; the next time he abandoned the bike for several days he went back to find it missing. Robert's bicycle career would probably have been terminated at this point except that three days later, as he was walking through the Piazza Augusto Imperatore on his way to the studio, what should he see but his old red bike secured with a brand new chain to a statue of Minerva. Without hesitation Robert rushed to his studio, seized a large metal saw and returned to attack the chain. Most of the good citizens of Rome walked by this odd spectacle, until a bus driver, spurred by a sense of civic responsibility, ventured to ask Robert what he meant by stealing that bicycle.

Robert was so enraged that he momentarily stopped sawing and launched into a diatribe aimed at the startled driver. Of course it was his bicycle, Robert roared. Would anyone but the owner want to steal such a terrible old wreck? He then proceeded to point

out to the driver all the dents and bruises that the bike had suffered in the last year. There on the fender was a dent it had got from a *cretino* taxi-driver. And look at the poor old light; he had personally strapped it to the wheel with a hand-bent piece of baling wire. It is possible that outrage, if it reaches true incandescence, can inflame others; for the driver regarded the angry Yank for several silent moments and then walked quickly away. Robert took his reclaimed bike immediately to his studio, and spent the next hour chiselling his name and phone number into the crossbar.

The next time the bike was stolen, the thief had the sense not to chain it to a post at Piazza Augusto Imperatore. That put the score in the Bicycle War at Thieves one, Robert zero.

At this point, there entered into Robert's circle a nice young man named Steven Potts, who had come to Italy to study sculpture with Robert. Potts was a bicycle enthusiast too. He had a green bike with good brakes and in short order he acquired a second, blue bike from a friend who was leaving for America. It goes without saying that Robert quickly offered to buy the blue bike for a token sum and wasted no time in chiselling name and telephone number into its bar.

Time passed. Robert put many miles on the blue bike, but one day he left it for a second on the pavement near the Pantheon while he was buying a special oil to kill scale insects on lemon trees.

'I was lazy. I didn't want to lean over and lock the chain,' Robert explained. 'I thought it would be OK if I just kept my eye on it through the window of the hardware store.' But when he next looked up the bicycle had gone. The Pantheon area is famous for such calamities. This brought the tally in the Bicycle Wars to Thieves two, Robert zero.

A few days of mourning followed, then Robert did a very unusual thing. He went out to a bike store and bought a beautiful black bike with five gears, a basket, a self-charging night light, and a bell so loud it terrified the cats on the Vicolo di Divino Amore. All for 275,000 lire. He also got, for 30,000 lire, a stout chain that looked like something used in the Inquisition to flail errant Catholics. So when Robert flashed around Rome on his errands to the Flower Market and the Carabinieri, he was not only speedy but also stylish.

At about this point, Potts had to return to America to take up his studies in architecture, so he offered to sell his excellent green bike to Robert. The sculptor first remarked that he already had an old blue bicycle but then he let drop the fact that he had never charged Potts for the sculpture lessons, so the green bicycle might be accepted in lieu of tuition fees. Potts brooded on this glumly and in the end the sculptor got the bike. Free. Bicycle thieves come in all shapes and colours. The score might now be considered Thieves two, Robert two.

The new black bicycle continued to be the chief means of transport as it was faster and also lighter than the old blue one, a factor of crucial importance as it had to be carried up three flights of stairs to the sculptor's flat in the evening, the *portiera* having withdrawn permission for it to stay overnight in the front lobby. But one Thursday around Easter it disappeared.

We were having lunch at Gioacchino's on the Via dei
Coronari – *spaghetti alle vongole* (spaghetti with
clams), *abbacchio al forno* (roast lamb), white wine
and salad – and when we came out Robert realized
that his bike, which he had chained to a billboard, was
gone. All that remained of it was the little brass
padlock, which had been neatly clipped open by a big
pair of wire-cutters.

Gloom and despair. Thieves three, Robert one.

Robert went straight round to his bicycle shop and
bought a great big triangular lock made of some
impregnable metal that could only be severed by a
team of arc-welders wearing gauntlets and goggles.
Cost, 70,000 lire.

'Finally,' said Robert with bitterness, 'I've got a
70,000-lire lock to protect a 30,000-lire old green bike.'
(Actually he had forgotten that the green bike had cost
him no lire at all.)

Two hours later, the phone rang and a gentleman
with a very courtly voice was on the line.

'If you are Robert Cook then I have your bicycle,' the
gentleman said. 'I was having coffee at a bar near my
negozio on the Via dei Banchi Vecchi just now when a
young kid offered to sell me this fancy black bicycle
for 100,000 lire. I could see your name engraved into
the metal. I bought it for 50,000 lire. When will you
come and fetch it?'

Three Italian friends advised us to have nothing to
do with this gentleman. He was obviously a fence,
they said. He had stolen the bicycle and 'he'll make
you pay through the nose to get it back. He might even
try to mug you.'

Robert rushed over to the Banchi Vecchi regardless (he was in such a hurry he wanted to ride the old green bike over, but I persuaded him it would be quicker to walk one way and ride back than to ride over and walk two bikes back), and the gentleman turned out to be even more charming than he sounded. He was an import-export dealer in trinkets, selling orange T-shirts from Taiwan, dolls that dribbled, watches with green faces, and mini-transistors that you pinned to your lapel and that told awful jokes.

He gave Robert the bike, plus a lapel-pin transistor, and stubbornly refused to take the 50,000 lire that Robert tried to press on him.

'Just invite me over for a drink some time,' he said.

I figure that makes it Thieves two, Robert two and a half, if you give half a point for the good will shown by the trinket salesman. Not only that, but the threat from bicycle thieves seemed to be dwindling with every passing day.

The scales were tilted against the thieves when Basque separatists tried to blow up the Palazzo Borghese across the street from us (there is a Spanish mission inside). All they succeeded in doing was blowing off the front door and breaking most of the windows in the piazza. This attack brought a carload of Carabinieri, armed with automatic weapons, who still park outside our front door twenty-four hours a day. And right next to them is a sturdy metal street lamp to which a bicycle can easily be chained.

With people like Robert around, Roman bicycle thieves had better start looking for a new profession.

CHAPTER SEVEN

The Backpack Set

LIVING IN THE CENTRE OF ROME CAN BE REWARDING BUT there are certain preliminary rules that must be understood before you can fully relax. We were, for instance, a bit slow in understanding the attraction of our three-bedroom apartment on Piazza Borghese. The tip-off came when we started to get letters from old classmates we hadn't seen since high school.

'We are so excited to hear you have moved into the centre of Old Rome,' wrote one classmate. 'It just happens that Roger and I are planning to be in Rome at Easter and we wondered if you could recommend a good place to stay in your area.' We recommended a pensione on the Piazza Nicosia.

But one afternoon in May back in the late 1960s Robert got a call from his mother in Boston to tell him that she had been working at the Buddies' Club reception centre for veterans of the Vietnam War and she had met two charming boys who had just been released from the services and were planning a trip through Italy. One was a fireman from Omaha, she said, and the other was a very nice boy from Maine, who was planning to finish his last year at college for a degree in electrical engineering.

'They are spending their discharge money on the trip,' she told Robert, 'so they can't afford very fancy hotels. I told them if they got into any trouble to call you, as you could always give them a bed for a night or two.'

'But, Ma,' Robert protested, 'we only have three bedrooms. Poor old Gina sleeps in a closet in the front hall already.'

'Well, I'm sure you can find someplace for them,' Mrs Cook said airily. 'After all, they've been fighting this dreadful war for us. They told me all they needed was a rug where they can put down their sleeping bags.'

The days passed and we worried quite a bit about what to do with Grandma's Vietnam veterans, and then one afternoon there was a ring on the buzzer and Gina went to answer.

She came back frowning.

'Signora, there are some foreigners buzzing our bell. *Non ne capisco proprio niente.* [I can't understand a word they say.]'

Sure enough, it was the veterans sent by Grandma Cook. I told them to come on up in the elevator and they appeared almost instantly, two young Americans wearing camouflage fatigues and carrying trunk-sized knapsacks, with rolled-up sleeping bags dangling from the sacks.

The huskier of the two came from Bangor, Maine, and had his dark hair clipped short in a military cut. His buddy from Omaha was slender with pale blue

eyes and blond hair curling around his ears. He had
that vague, innocent look that is often attractive to
girls of twenty.

'Welcome to Rome,' I said cheerfully after they had
introduced themselves. 'What can I do for you two?'

The two immediately hunched their shoulders and
lowered their fifty-pound sacks to the floor.

'Well, as long as you asked,' said the first, 'what we
need is a big glass of water. We've been walking
around all day and the thirst is getting to us.'

I led them to the fridge in the kitchen, and they
looked admiringly at the rooms along the corridor.

'Boy, you've got a really great place,' said one with
wonder. 'This is the nicest place we've seen since we
left the States. Hey, Bronson?' His friend nodded.

'It's not really *that* big,' I said. 'We have two children

and the maid. So we need three rooms for us, and one for Gina.'

There was a moment's pause as we all looked at one another and already I felt guilty.

The bigger one, David, who was clearly the patrol leader, looked me straight in the eye.

'We don't need a room,' he said with a great show of sincerity. 'We told Mrs Cook that we'd be just as happy to spread out on a rug anywhere. We won't be in Rome long. We're on our way to Positano.'

I hesitated. 'How long might that be?' I asked. I didn't want to seem inhospitable.

'Only a couple of days,' said David.

'Yeah, just a couple,' echoed his friend.

'Well, if that's the case, let's see what rug to give you.'

I explained that the front entrance might be the best place, because there was already one bed there and they could take turns, but they surveyed the entrance and shook their heads.

'No, ma'am,' said David, 'we don't want to take your last bed. Maybe there's someplace else.'

So I led them on a tour of the house and they showed more interest in the living room.

'At least here we would be out of the way,' David remarked, looking at the television set and the door to the terrace.

I did not have the heart to tell them that the living room was not all that convenient. But his friend stepped out to the terrace and liked what he saw.

'Hey, David, this is just the place for us. We can put our sacks out here and we won't bother anyone.'

The idea of two veterans sleeping on our terrace under the bright skies and the bright eyes of Rome seemed a bit much to me, but I could think of no real reason to object. So by the time the children came home from school they found two husky Vietnam veterans unpacking their bags in our living room while they watched a soccer match on our television set.

'But what are those two soldiers doing watching our TV?' asked Henry, who was now seven.

I tried to explain to him that they were veterans who had fought a hard war on our behalf, and that we had to be nice to them.

Later in the afternoon, when the soccer game was over, our new guests asked if they could possibly take a shower.

'It's been a week since we had a real shower, and I'm afraid we really need one,' David said.

Naturally I assented to this modest request. I gave the boys two towels and they disappeared into the bathroom, to emerge forty minutes later wearing relief jeans and clutching their damp towels wrapped around rolls of sodden clothing.

'We took advantage of the hot water to do some laundry. We can just hang these things to dry on the terrace, OK?'

Since it was not Tuesday, which was our day to dry laundry on the upper terrace, I nodded acquiescence. Then I watched as the two draped their khaki underwear on our flowering lemon trees.

An hour later I met our neighbour Maresciallo Palinetti.

'Signora! What are those soldiers doing hanging their clothes on your beautiful lemon trees? They are American, no?'

His question had a semi-official tone. With reproach in his voice he reminded me of an old Italian law that decreed that if you entertained foreigners in your rented apartments for even one night, you were obliged to report them to the Office for Foreigners at the Questura.

I tried to explain that the two boys were old friends of Robert's mother, almost relatives in fact. We felt it was our duty to show them hospitality, but only for a day or so of course.

Somewhat mollified, the Maresciallo moved on, suggesting that after two days we should give him the names of the guests so that he could report them to the Questura, thus saving us *un mare di guai* (a sea of troubles).

We were now approaching dinner time, and Gina came to ask me if the two 'soldiers' would stay for

supper. All she had planned, Gina said, was *spaghetti al pesto* and salad.

Again I was a coward.

'Well, that's no trouble, Gina. Just add some more spaghetti and a big mixed salad and we'll have a nice supper for six.'

So when Robert came home from the studio, he found the two guests stretched on the floor watching a quiz programme on the TV, while Henry helped translate for them and Gina cooked spaghetti for six.

The boys were happy to join us at dinner and finished off their spaghetti and salad in a very short time. Realizing that a single dish of spaghetti might be a bit on the light side, I went to the kitchen to see what else we might offer. There I discovered a packet of special raw Parma ham that Gina had bought for lunch the next day, so I took it to the table, and the two guests availed themselves of a basket of fresh rolls to make ham sandwiches. When they had finished, the ham was finished too.

Robert, never one to rest on ceremony, turned to the boys as soon as we got up from the table.

'Just how long are you fellows planning to stay in Rome?' he asked.

Even as I fled the room I heard David saying, 'Oh, not long at all really. We're on our way to the Amalfi coast, but first we have to find our friend in Positano who is going to put us up.'

'Well, why don't you call him up then?' Robert said, pointing to the telephone. 'Make a call on me.'

I was not present when the two got through to Positano but Robert reported to me that, after trying several times, they found that the friend they were looking for had gone to Capri for a few days.

'I asked them if he was coming back, and they were a little vague about that. I wouldn't put it beyond these two to hang on here for a couple of days. I explained to them that if they stayed another day, it would be better if they went out to eat because Gina had to do a lot of laundry and already had enough on her hands.'

'I wonder about that friend in Positano,' I said. 'When I talked to them earlier this afternoon they also mentioned some friends in Genoa.'

'Right,' said Robert. 'Maybe we are just a holding station until something better shows up.'

We left our friends watching the television about eleven o'clock that night, and we wished them a happy time sleeping on our terrace. When we came in for breakfast, we found them sleeping on our living-room rug.

'What happened?'

'Too much noise,' David murmured. 'First there were the cats, and then there was the restaurant closing up. All the cooks and waiters were out in the back alley playing soccer. So we finally moved indoors. Hope you don't mind if we sleep a little longer.'

In the end the two went back to their sleeping bags and slept until eleven, when they decided to take another shower.

'I'm surprised you are not in a hurry to get out and see Rome,' I remarked as they emerged from the bath-room. 'I suggest you telephone your friends first and then go out and visit the Vatican.'

The two looked disconsolate, but they did put in several telephone calls with no apparent results, and then reluctantly set off to see the sights of Rome. They were back in the flat at two thirty, anxious for a beer and a nap in the living room. Once awake, they turned on the television again.

By the time Robert got home for dinner it was obvious that our guests had no intention of leaving soon. So he lowered the boom.

'Look, my friends, I have to go to the country to plant some trees and do some cutting, and I thought you might like to come out with me and help.'

The two looked glumly at each other, and then David gave an almost imperceptible nod. 'Yeah, I suppose that's an idea,' he said in a low voice.

An hour later the two had collected their laundry and packed their knapsacks, and soon they were rolling out to the country in our faithful Morris Minor. Two days later Robert called from Sora Giulia's restaurant in Quadroni.

'Well, our heroes are on their way,' he said. 'They were actually quite a help cutting down some of those old oaks on the border. The thin blond one, the fireman, turned out to be a whizz with the chainsaw. I think he used chainsaws trying to rescue farmers from burning barns and forest fires. He could get the saw going with just one pull on the rope; he has a very strong right arm. Then he would make a slice one way in a trunk, and another cut making a V, and the tree would fall exactly where he wanted it to fall. I told them to stay around to help me as long as they liked, but they said they had to be going as their friends were expecting them. When we got to the train station I asked them where they were heading, and one of them said Positano and the other said Genoa. So I guess they are still trying to make up their minds.'

CHAPTER EIGHT

La Portiera

ROMANS TEND TO BE SUSPICIOUS PEOPLE. MANY OF THEM keep a certain distance from the *portiere* of their buildings because they are convinced that they are spies for the police. There may be something to this fear, but I suspect that the *portiere*'s duties have gradually dwindled into something less dramatic than spying. They are responsible for opening and closing the main doors of the building morning and night, keeping the halls and stairs clean, and ensuring that the mail is distributed in the right boxes.

Having suffered under unpleasant *portiere* in other buildings, I was surprised but also delighted when we moved into Piazza Borghese to discover that our new *portiera* was a cheerful woman who ran a kind of permanent coffee bar for her friends in the neighbourhood. Anyone who was so popular, I thought, could not have much time or inclination to spy for the police.

Angela, for that was her name, hailed from Frosinone and had come to Rome in the immediate post-war years to take her first job as a *tuttofare* in our building at 8,000 lire a month. Eventually she had attracted the attention of the *portiere* of the building, an upstanding gentleman named Arcibaldo, who had been widowed at the age of sixty-two. After she had been working in the building for about a year, Arcibaldo surprised everyone by asking Angela to marry him. Angela accepted with alacrity, not only because Arcibaldo was very *signorile* (gentlemanly) and *sobrio* (sober) but also because the move from *tuttofare* to *portiera* was a promotion for her. An unexpected but most felicitous outcome of this marriage was the birth of a baby boy, Gigio, and both parents were as pleased as could be. Sadly, four years after Gigio's birth Arcibaldo had a heart attack and died, leaving Angela with a smallish son but also a secure job as *portiera* in the palazzo.

I couldn't help comparing her life with that of a janitor in the United States. In Italy in the Sixties and Seventies, people who had dullish jobs and minimum prospects did not seem to consider themselves defeated, as did their counterparts in Manhattan. As an American sage once put it, 'There came a time in mid-century America when people began to be labelled either as "successes" or "failures", and as a result, a lot of people were rendered very unhappy.' In Italy I don't think this line was drawn so firmly, and people tended to settle comfortably into their lives no matter what their prospects.

I enjoyed the gossip down in Angela's place. A favourite subject was La Signorina Nicolosi, a rather bird-like spinster of about fifty who had taken a big flat on the top floor and proceeded to rent out rooms to a

series of unattached working gentlemen, who were accepted on the clear understanding that they would invite no guests into their rooms. Angela knew very well that renting out rooms was illegal in our building, but since she was a kindly soul she never reported the matter to our landlord, La Cattolica. She was further amused by the fact that despite her rigid moral stance with others, La Signorina had for years been the mistress of one of her most distinguished lodgers, who played first violin in a prestigious orchestra and had the room next to La Signorina in the apartment. The idea of a clandestine relationship between these two prim and proper souls was a cause for no little hilarity downstairs.

Once we had exhausted the matter of the sexy signorina, we often got around to the subject closest to Angela's heart: how was she to find a good wife for her beloved son Gigio? At the time of our arrival Gigio was already twenty-three. He was a tidy young man with curly hair and dark eyes but there was something old-fashioned and over-formal about him. In an era when laid-back, casual manners seemed to be the thing, Gigio was almost too polite. I suspected that Angela had brought him up with the idea that he would be the *portiere* some day, and so she had tried to instil in him qualities that she thought a *portiere* should have – quietness, obedience, reliability – qualities that we now find only in the butlers in old-fashioned English movies.

Gigio seemed to have little personal ambition. Since he was not needed to help his mother in the building, he had found a job as a delivery boy on a Vespa for the department store Tebro, which was only a block away. This was surely not a brilliant start to his career but the fact that he stood to inherit a *portinerato* (a porter's job) in a big palazzo in central Rome was an undoubted attraction, and a number of young ladies in the area had set their caps at him. One who seemed especially persistent was a second cousin named Rita, who came from Angela's home town of Frosinone and was living with an aunt and uncle near Piazza Navona. Rita was admittedly older than Gigio and, as Angela often pointed out, she was also a touch on the heavy side. On the other hand she was bright and cheerful and it seemed to me (but not Angela) that she might provide some of the spontaneous qualities that Gigio was lacking.

But Angela would have none of it – an attitude that she was to regret in the years ahead.

'I don't want my Gigio to be marrying one of those country girls from Frosinone,' she said. 'There are lots of girls in Rome who are younger and prettier and would make good wives for my son.'

But none of these girls worked out. So one summer Gigio and Angela went to Frosinone for two weeks, and when they came back Angela announced that Gigio had found a girl he liked. Her name was Monica and they were going to be married in a month's time. The young couple returned to Rome in late September, and Robert, who fancies himself a judge of beauteous womanhood, was not impressed.

'You can take a girl out of Frosinone,' he announced, 'but you can't take Frosinone out of the girl.'

There was something in what Robert said. Monica had a country look about her. She was built *con culo per terra* (bottom on the ground) with strong legs and turned-out toes; she had a mop of frizzy hair that defied any attempt to flatten it. There was an aggressive look in her eye, and none of the uncertainty that you often find in a young country girl. Gina, who had dropped by to meet the new arrival, was full of foreboding.

'That girl is a *prepotente* [bully],' she complained. 'She will give poor Angela a lot of trouble.'

The girl did not show her true colours in the next few years as she was busy learning about the building and helping Angela with some of the chores. From the first her attitude was quite different from that of her mother-in-law. Whenever Gina asked her for a key to the top-floor terrace to hang out laundry there was always a problem. Monica would explain that the key was not available that day because La Signora Scarpa had just hung her sheets there or because La Signorina Nicolosi had a huge load of washing to dry, which was not surprising as she had five or six male boarders who changed their shirts every day. The signorina also used the terrace in warm weather to dry out rolled-up balls of wet newspaper, which she was accustomed to burn instead of coal in her stove.

'Monica is also a *ruffiana* [flirt],' Gina complained one day. 'Every time one of the workers comes to fix the water tanks on the roof, she goes up to help him, and she is smiling and laughing as if he were her *fidanzato* [boyfriend]. She forgets she is a married woman.'

There were also difficult days when it rained, so we had to double up with Monica's laundry too, and inevitably by the end of the day Monica had pushed all of our wash onto one corner of the line, so that hers could get the full sun.

'You'll see,' Gina said darkly, 'that girl from Frosinone is going to cause trouble all round.'

The blow came sooner than we expected. One day in early spring I stopped at the *portiera*'s office on my way out to give Angela a book to pass to a friend. As I held it out to Angela, Monica snatched it.

'Signora, don't give anything to Angela,' she said abruptly. 'I am the *portiera* now.'

I looked at Angela with surprise, but she avoided my glance.

Gina had the story for me in the evening.

'You won't believe me, but that *bisbetica* [shrew] has tricked Angela out of her job, and she has tricked that poor foolish Gigio too.'

The story was that Monica, to augment the family income, had taken a job cleaning for an architect who lived on the top floor and who happened to be a director of La Cattolica. The Cattolica had a habit of renting out apartments at friendly rates to top-rank employees. Monica had played up to this gentleman, doing his shopping for him and bringing his newspaper in the morning, and in the end she had persuaded him that since Angela had reached retirement age she would be eligible for a good pension, and she, Monica, should take over the job of *portiera* at once. She explained that the building needed a younger, more aggressive hand at the helm, and because of her ability to add up long columns of figures she would be better at the job than her husband Gigio.

When the *portiera*'s contract came up for renewal, Monica's friend the architect upstairs had managed to alter the text before signature. It appeared Angela had not fully understood the working of the document and had signed on the understanding that she would receive her pension at once and be able to live in the *portinaio* for the rest of her life. She was also assured by Monica that Gigio was happy to continue his job as delivery boy, so that the family could benefit from two salaries instead of one.

Gina tried to persuade Angela that she had been tricked into this unexpected retirement. But Angela was assured by the director that everything would remain the same; she could go on as before, assisted by a younger woman, and the family income would benefit. An optimistic scenario indeed. Monica took over the *portiera*'s duties with a vengeance and things changed with alacrity. Instead of a full day to dry clothes on the terrace, we were all reduced to half a day once a week. Soon after this she posted a notice in the front hall, informing us all that her office would be closed 'according to the law' from twelve noon until 2 p.m. every day and that she would be 'off duty' during that period. Accordingly, if any special mail or packages were delivered during the lunch hour, the deliveries would be refused and recipients would have to fetch them from the post office two days later.

After six months the strain was too much for Angela and she decided to pack up and go to live with her widowed sister in Frosinone. She confided in Gina that her daughter-in-law had evicted her from her bedroom, so that her own mother could come to visit her, and Angela was forced to sleep in a dank basement bedroom underneath the *portiera*'s office. Her pension cheques also turned out to be less than expected.

The atmosphere in the *portiera*'s office became more and more oppressive.

Gigio began to look harassed and worried. Soon Gina reported that Monica and Gigio were getting a legal separation and he had gone to live with his mother. To keep his job at the department store, he now had to make a two-hour commute by bus each day from Frosinone to Rome and back.

Simultaneously, Monica started keeping company with a glum-looking man who worked as a gilder in a nearby picture-framing shop. Often on Saturday mornings he came to fetch Monica in his Alfa Romeo and they would go for weekends to his cottage near the sea in Ladispoli.

Over the months, Monica had managed to acquire considerable power over most of the tenants in the building. She frequently closed the *portone* (main door) on Fridays too, leaving us all without post from Thursday to Monday. And every time we tried dropping the rubbish off before 7 p.m. as we were going out to dinner we would hear a harsh 'Signora!' from her door, and would be reminded that we were not allowed to leave our rubbish until 8 p.m. 'Take it anywhere you want,' she called. 'Throw it in the side alley next to the church, just so it isn't in my building.'

Then there was one afternoon in June when she summoned me to her office and held out a small sheaf of papers for me to sign. 'Routine paperwork,' she said. I sat down in her chair and flipped through the papers and discovered towards the bottom of page two that tenants who signed were agreeing to 'assume responsibility' for a two-month period in summer, when a 'supplementary functionary' would come in to handle the mail. It turned out the 'petition' was Monica's attempt to get herself a long summer holiday, with the unwitting tenants picking up the bill for her two-month replacement.

When I enquired of the lady if she had cleared this matter with La Cattolica, she replied that this was actually an agreement between her and the tenants at Piazza Borghese 91, and there was no need to tell the Cattolica people. When I heard this, I returned the papers to her explaining that I would have to consult with Robert, and I warned several other tenants of the *imbroglio* and they also refused to sign. Monica was vastly displeased.

There was in addition the recurrent problem of her nephew, Giorgio, who often came from Frosinone on his stripped-down motorcycle to spend the weekend with his aunt in Rome. Giorgio wore black jeans and a black leather jacket, and had his hair clipped in a 'Nazi-skin' cut. Marcello, our newsagent across the street, explained to me that Giorgio was a typical *teppista* (hooligan) from the country, who came to Rome to involve himself in whatever trouble he could find on the city streets at night – soccer dust-ups or political skirmishes or even a little purse-snatching. But often his activities were limited because of the breakdown of his motorcycle.

One cold winter night when we were getting ready for bed, there was a dreadful revving of motor-cycles on the Vicolo di San Biagio. We looked out and could see two dark figures working hard to repair an engine. Since it was past midnight I leaned out of the window and called, '*Basta*. We are sleeping.'

The figures paid no attention to us and went on revving, so then Robert yelled at them to go away or he would call the Carabinieri. Still no reaction from the two figures. At this point I went to the kitchen and filled a big bucket with water, took it to the open window and pitched it at the figures. I aimed well and the water caught them both, drenching their heads and shoulders. At this point the boys, one of whom was clearly Giorgio, started yelling back at us in outraged tones, but we simply shut the window and went to bed. The two apparently chained their motorcycles to a nearby lamp post and disappeared. The alley was quiet for the night.

The next morning as I was going to collect the mail, a stern voice from the *portiera*'s office summoned me.

'Signora!' It was Monica. 'Signora, did you throw water on Giorgio last night?'

The coward in me suggested that I could deny the assault. But I knew this would be a mistake. 'Of course I threw the water,' I said sternly. 'They were keeping the whole neighbourhood awake after midnight.'

'Aha,' she said. 'It was a very cold night, and the cold water on their heads may give them *bronchopolmonite*. Or worse.'

For the next year the *portiera* and I never exchanged a word. The situation deteriorated, and eventually one Christmas Robert said, 'We can't go on like this. I'm going to give the witch a tip this year and see what happens.'

Since he didn't want to talk to her, he tucked 100,000 lire into an envelope and put it in her mailbox. The next morning as I went out, she greeted me with a warm smile and thanked me cordially for *il pensiero* (the thought).

Suddenly our mail was all put neatly in our box every day, and if we received a larger package she kept it in her office without complaint and left us a note to pick it up. We gave her another tip at Easter. Then, throwing caution to the winds, we left her money at Ferragosto, the mid-August holiday, which is also celebrated with gracious giving.

Monica's change of heart wasn't a flash in the pan. We now have a *portiera* who greets us cheerfully every morning, enquires after our health, and even presents me with a potted clivia at Easter. As the TV comic Renzo Arbore put it so wisely, '*Meditate, gente, meditate.*' We are meditating.

CHAPTER NINE

Skeletons under Our Terrace

ONE IMPORTANT LESSON I LEARNED IN TERRACE gardening is that you should never trust anyone to water the terrace when you are away. Neighbours will promise to help but invariably something unforeseen, like a sick child or a visiting uncle, distracts them. In the end you are forced to fall back on the reluctant *portiera*, but since she is basically doing you a favour, you have no right to complain if she manages to apply water for five minutes only every other day. When you arrive home after a ten-day absence, even if your flowers look up at you wilted and outraged, you must thank her for keeping your terrace alive.

In the end it was Gina's socialist nephew Piero who set us up with a good watering system of sprinklers and drippers, and thermostats and timers that could be set to go on and off several times a day. Like all other technical systems, it took me nearly a week to conquer, but I finally discovered that if I followed some hand-written instructions I could set it going full tilt for about six months of the year – from May to October – and slowly reduce the water in the cooler months until the plants were getting a small amount once a week.

The system is not foolproof, but on the other hand it has never brought us any real disasters. (It has never, for instance, turned itself on and kept going for two weeks, flooding the entire building, a tragedy which all of my Roman friends assured me was bound to happen sooner or later. Nor has it ever capriciously closed down, bringing instant desertification.)

My problems are more commonplace. Once in a while the big blackbird who runs a harem on the rooftop of the Chiesa del Divino Amore comes over with one of his girlfriends and pecks about in the pots looking for worms or fresh manure. The birds sometimes manage to turf out one of the little water sprinklers, leaving a pot completely without water, and only if it's spotted quickly can the plant be saved. There is also the danger of cigarette butts and the odd beer can tossed down by our criminologist neighbour, the professor, a floor above us. But the worst menace of all comes from the owners of our building, La Cattolica, who suffer from a recurring fixation that the watering system on our terrace is the cause of all the leaking and flooding that occurs on our side of the building.

As a result, we have suffered several terrace-remodelling jobs. The first was caused by Signora Scarpa on the floor below, who complained to the landlord that water from our terrace was seeping through her ceiling and causing great damage to her oriental rug, an heirloom of inestimable value. We had always been on good terms with the signora. Her affectionate nature extended to cats and pigeons in the neighbourhood, and to show her love for them she regularly threw crumbs and bits of leftover spaghetti onto the roof of the church, in the mistaken belief that it would help feed the two cats who frequented it. In actual fact, these roof cats, who never ventured down to street level where the thuggish street cats hang out, were extremely well fed at home, and weren't even slightly interested. Like the cats, the pigeons could also take the bread or leave it, but the animals who got the most out of it were the church mice, who dis-covered these supplies on the roof and moved from their headquarters in the church itself up to the roof, creating a sort of mousery right next door to the open terrace where the nuns hang out their washing. This assemblage of mice soon attracted all kinds of raptors. Suddenly, blackbirds, crows and even shrieking flocks of seagulls seemed to take over Rome.

But to get back to our terrace: La Cattolica sent us a letter stating that, due to Signora Scarpa's complaint, our terrace had to be completely dug up, rendered waterproof and then replaced, but before this could be done we would be required to remove all the pots from it. Obedient as seeing-eye dogs, we hefted all the pots, about a hundred of them including two very heavy lemon trees, up the three steps and into our living room, which also sported a less important Persian rug. We rolled up the rug and covered most of the floor with torn sheets, and for three full weeks our living room became a make-do greenhouse. Naturally, keeping plants happy and well watered in a living room was no easy job; as the pots leaked, the lemons started to shed their fruit, and all the plants suffered mightily from being cramped up in a tight and sunless space.

The work of stopping this leak seemed endless. Five hefty Abruzzi workmen had to rip up the old terrace tiles, using pick-axes and pneumatic drills that sent clouds of cement dust into our living room. Most of this broken masonry was then evacuated down the side of the building on a rustic pulley system, where it was unloaded again. All of this operation required a lot of yelling and hallooing from our third floor to the street level, and the ensuing hubbub made conversation at lunch well-nigh impossible. And whenever there were really big items to bring upstairs – great rolls of tar paper, crates of heavy terracotta tiles or buckets of liquid bitumen – the pulley wouldn't do the job, so the builders had to bring them up in the lift and then heft them about sixty metres down our narrow corridor and through the dining room and living room to reach the terrace.

These portages began about seven in the morning and went on until five in the afternoon, with an hour off at midday, and the constant ringing of the doorbell became so annoying that we finally left the front door ajar. This open-door policy meant, of course, that as we returned from the bath in dressing gowns with heads in towels we were liable to run into sweating Abruzzi workers with great buckets of nails, or *pozzolana* (cement and lime) on their shoulders. We also frequently collided with a waiter from the café across the street, carrying a tray of espresso coffee for the officials of Regione Veneto, whose offices, he had failed to realize, were on the floor below us.

I don't know how it is in other countries, but if you

have workers in your home in Italy you are gradually converted into a sort of involuntary workers' helper – a *manovale* (manual worker) who does all the hod-carrying and cleaning-up. First a *muratore* (mason) needs a Phillips screwdriver, which he seems to have forgotten; then he asks you if you happen to have a shovel, or a jug of cold water because his throat is dry, or a cachet of aspirin because he has a migraine. In thanks for your kindness, you will find him using your best wrought-iron terrace furniture as an impromptu stepladder, and he will mix his special tile cement in your nicest copper plant container.

The workers also found it natural to clean themselves up in the late afternoon by using our priceless watering system as a shower. We ended up with grit in our beds, broken rungs on our ladder, and a bent terrace chair that they had attempted to convert into a carpenter's bench – also, a broken watering system. All this meant that when the plants were returned to their rightful places on the terrace, they were in such terrible shape that it seemed almost useless to try to revive them. We subsequently found that instant revival was out of the question anyhow because our water wizard, smiling Piero, had taken off for a three-week holiday on Stromboli.

Things were just beginning to return to normal four months later, when I received a telephone call from a lady at La Cattolica. A new leak had developed onto Signora Scarpa's oriental rug, she said, but not to worry: this time they had decided that the leak might be either under our terrace stairs or connected with the drainage pipes. This would therefore require one corner of the terrace floor to be lifted up again, so that pipes could be found and leaks stopped.

'You understand, of course,' she said, 'that you will have to remove plants located around the pipes.'

I made an effort to keep my voice level. 'No, we cannot remove the plants a second time. You will have to work around them,' I said.

She quickly pointed out in a menacing tone that if necessary she could get a court order to make us remove the plants.

'That would be a mistake,' I replied, 'because if you are talking about law you people at La Cattolica have broken the zoning laws of the city which stipulate that this building should remain a residential building. Instead you are renting out the ground floor to a commercial restaurant.' I was referring to the Rome branch of the famous El Toula restaurant that took up half of the ground floor of our building, and whose kitchen opened straight onto the Vicolo di San Biagio, directly below all of our bedrooms. I pointed out that this kitchen, where ten or twelve Venetian cooks worked, was the noisiest spot in central Rome, and completely destroyed the sleep of all the local residents.

'It would be one thing if it was a business that worked indoors, like an accountant's office,' I said, 'but the cooks and waiters at El Toula are a group of madmen and think nothing of starting a noisy soccer match in the back alley at two in the morning. They play their radios at top volume, and also run a kind of outdoor refreshment stand at the kitchen window from midnight, serving free drinks and raw ham to their girlfriends and other street bums.' I then mentioned the rattling refuse truck that came round every night as soon as El Toula closed, and the four refuse collectors who didn't just pick up the rubbish and dump it quietly into the bottom of the truck; they grabbed the empty bottles one by one and pitched them hard onto the truck's metal floor, where they exploded like grenades.

When I had stopped for breath, the lady at La Cattolica broke in to suggest in a conciliatory tone that the men who would be doing the repair work on the terrace would be mainly digging up pipes, not flooring, and she would ask them to help us lug the larger plants to our living room.

I will not go into the agonies of our second worker invasion except to say that there were fewer plants in the living room this time, because many of my original plants were dead. We therefore were able to go ahead with our lives in a more civilized fashion. But suddenly at lunchtime on the fifth day, we realized that we had not heard any noise at all from the workers for several hours. We peered out of our window to the Vicolo di San Biagio to discover four police vehicles, their lights flashing, and near them police officers were busy roping off the area with yellow plastic cords to keep people out. A small crowd, including a number of cooks from El Toula, were standing in their doorway idly watching, and across the street three nuns from the Chiesa del Divino Amore were peering through polyester curtains from their second-floor window.

I went downstairs to investigate, but the police were in no mood to let me pass.

'*Non si passa,*' said one solemn Carabinieri officer. '*È una cosa seria, molto seria.* [It is a very serious matter.]'

'What is it exactly?'

He lowered his eyes from a point he had been focusing on just above my head.

'*Omicidio,*' he said, '*omicidio in un armadio* [murder in a wardrobe].'

After dropping that bomb he walked away. I eased over to stand next to a cook from El Toula, whom I recognized as one of the leaders of the midnight revelries.

'*Che succede?*'

He decided my question was a valid one, so he turned to me. 'The building workers were pulling out an old pipe that went through the bedroom of the *pellicciaia* [furrier] on the first floor, and they knocked open the door of an old wooden *armadio*. Inside they found a skeleton, and they believe it is the bones of the *pellicciaia*'s sister, a certain Immaculata, who disappeared two years ago. They have already charged the *pellicciaia* with murder.'

'You mean the body has been sitting in that *armadio* for two years?'

The cook smiled grimly, as if he'd found a toad in the tortellini. 'When it got very hot last summer, I used to sit outside making the chicken aspic and vichyssoise and I used to smell some strange aroma coming from that window.'

The papers ran the story for about three days, but since the sisters were neither showgirls nor the lovers of leading politicians but simply two eccentric spinsters who made a living sewing new chinchilla collars onto old mink coats, nobody seemed to care if they were dead or alive.

For the next week the alley below our terrace was roped off and our workers were not allowed to repair the leaky pipes. At the beginning of the second week a small item in the *Messaggero* said that the Roman procurator had closed the case in a hurry. His verdict? The dead sister had died of causes unknown. The living one was then assigned to a state institution on the far side of Monte Mario.

The uncaring Cattolica quickly sent in a worker who threw all the odd bits and pieces of ermine, beaver and

sable into plastic bags and took them away, and then applied a coat of whitewash over the tired old walls. The furrier's place was then rented out at a fancy fee to a bright young computer programmer with designer stubble and Gucci loafers. I don't think anyone in the building ever told him about the skeleton.

It transpired that the leak onto the Bokhara rug had stopped at about the same time as the skeleton was uncovered, and it was assumed that the original leak had been caused by a block of some sort in the exit tube that ran by the old *armadio*. The workers came back only long enough to pack up their tools and lug our plants out onto the terrace again. I realized at this point that we were missing several plants, including a rare variegated elephant ear plant that I had brought from Kerala. Our automatic watering system, so good for late afternoon showers, was broken once again. Still, from a distance the terrace didn't look too bad. We began the joyous job of replanting it all two days later.

II

FRIENDS AND FLOWER PEOPLE

Friends

~

Neighbours

~

Cat ladies

~

Unusual gardeners

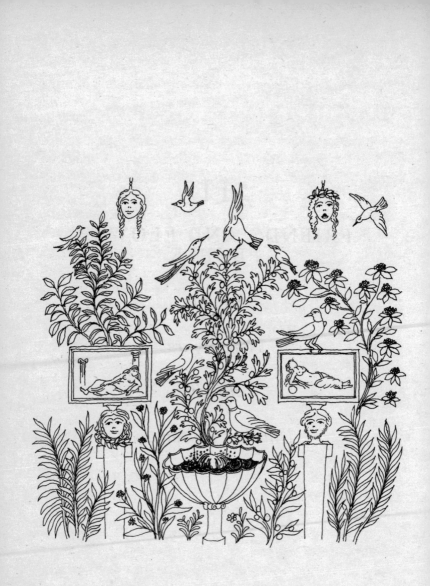

Once we had settled in, we were free to reach out and meet the people. As expatriates we soon became friendly with other foreigners in Rome, but I am happy to say that this did not exclude warm relationships with Italians as well, especially those who had travelled or studied abroad, or had interests that went beyond their own intimate family concerns. We realized in time that many of the best friends we made in Rome were couples where one of the partners was Italian and the other a foreigner. There is nothing like marriage to an outlander to broaden horizons, both culturally and emotionally.

Since gardening and ecology were of great interest to me and I was writing on the Italian gardening scene, we gradually came to know a number of people who shared these concerns, not only in Italy but all over the planet. Accordingly, the middle section that follows focuses mostly on the people I encountered in this way. I start with two foreigners, one from Mobile, Alabama, and one from Liverpool, England, who created delightful terraces on the rooftops above Rome.

After joining the Garden Club of Rome, I came to know many Italian women who were deeply involved with gardens. Among them were two Caetani princesses, a mother and daughter, who developed the great Caetani estate at Ninfa into one of the most beautiful gardens in the land. I also came to know and admire some less famous ladies, two of whom created a unique ecological niche in the harsh and dangerous soil of Mafia-ridden Palermo, and two other ladies in Rome who showed me how to break the old rules about rose gardening.

I was also lucky to meet some excellent male gardeners, one an English lord who is completely remodelling an abandoned Chigi garden near Siena, and the other an Australian expat who has developed the most extensive herb-garden nursery in Italy.

CHAPTER TEN

Eugene and the Post-war Revival

MOST OF US WHO CAME TO ROME IN THE POST-WAR years liked to believe that Rome in the early Fifties was a kind of replica of Paris in the Twenties and Thirties. It will remain for future historians to decide if the excitement we felt was justified.

Almost as soon as hostilities had ceased in 1945, a goodly number of British artists and writers began the trek to Italy. Early arrivals included the English writers Graham Greene and George Orwell. The American influx was far larger and took longer as the Yanks had to travel to Europe in very old and very slow ships, while the faster means of transport were still engaged in bringing troops home from the war. (It is seldom remembered that it was not until 1958 that aeroplanes began carrying more passengers across the Atlantic than ships did.) American writers who came to Rome in those years included Sinclair Lewis, John Steinbeck, Mary McCarthy, Gore Vidal, Ralph Ellison, William Styron and Tennessee Williams. Among the prominent painters who joined the exodus was William de Kooning.

The bulk of the Americans who came to Italy were not famous names but unknown poets, writers and artists (including Robert), whose travel was subsidized to a large degree by two enlightened laws passed by the US Congress. One was the Fulbright Law, which gave special grants to selected artists who showed promise. The other law, the GI Bill of Rights, was a far more inclusive piece of legislation that provided funding to all American war veterans who wished to continue their education after the war. A surprising number took a year or two in Europe to decide what they wanted to do with their lives, and many of them chose to continue their careers in the arts, which they never would have done without the GI Bill. The benefit to the US arts scene was incalculable.

New York chroniclers like to talk about the great 'Golden Age' that followed the Second World War in New York City, presided over by the likes of Truman Capote and Andy Warhol. As golden ages go, however, the Warhol Age had more to do with publicity and gossip than it had to do with art. For even while these New York celebrities were tearing up and down the slippery slope to instant fame, we Romans found ourselves being energized and entertained by some of our own more amusing and more talented minstrel men.

One of the most captivating of all these (and a focus for much of the foreign colony in Rome) was a youngish artist and writer named Eugene Walter, who came from Mobile, Alabama, by way of three years' war service in an ice-bound US base in the Aleutian Islands off Alaska. Gore Vidal, who also served in the Aleutians, wrote about Eugene, 'Truman Capote lied to harm others; Eugene Walter, sometimes known as the other Capote – the good one – lied only to delight others.' Another fan of Eugene, the author Muriel Spark, said of him, 'Eugene Walter held the nearest thing to a salon in Rome; he was an unofficial reception committee and all roads led to him.'

Luckily one of my roads – through an iris garden – led me straight to Eugene very early on, and I recognized at once that I was in the presence of a true Renaissance figure. I first met him out on the Appia Antica visiting Signora Monica Sgaravatti's iris garden. Signora Sgaravatti was an iris hybridizer and every May for two weeks she opened her garden to all Roman iris-lovers.

The signora was a tall no-nonsense lady in her mid-fifties who generally wore a blue smock with purpose-designed pockets, one to hold a pair of pruning shears and another for a small trowel. The third was a detachable pocket with buttons which served as a catch-all for faded iris flowers. As she led visiting groups around the garden, Signora Monica would stop when she saw a stalk with faded flowers, nip them off with her shears and pop them into the pocket. Later, I assumed, a maid removed the whole pocket and dumped the tired blooms.

As we toured her garden on my first visit I noticed that our hostess was being closely followed by a jolly-looking youngish American, who was wearing a beige linen suit with a white rose in his buttonhole and an off-white Panama hat. He walked right behind the signora, who was moving fast, and he listened to every word she said and occasionally made notes in a small notebook. The signora saw that he was playing close attention and turned to engage him in conversation.

'You seem very interested in irises,' she said. 'Do you grow them yourself?'

'I do,' the young man replied promptly. 'I have about twenty kinds of new German iris on my terrace in Rome this very moment.'

The signora looked at him with disbelief. 'On a terrace! In Rome! I do not believe you. You cannot grow iris on a terrace!'

The young man smiled a pussy-cat smile. 'If you don't believe me, come and see.' He said this in good Italian, spiced by a strong southern accent.

'But what kind do you grow?' she asked with curiosity. 'I suppose they are the common purple ones and the blue Florentine ones [gaggioli].'

That was her way of saying that if he did grow iris on his terrace it would be one of the weedy types that flower beside country roads all over Tuscany.

'Not at all, signora,' he responded. 'I grow some very pale blue iris I got from Denmark that are far paler than your "Blue Ice", and I also have two or three pink and purple iris which you do not have at all.'

The lady blinked. 'I cannot believe that you can grow these on a terrace. I have never heard such a thing.' Her voice was developing an edge to it. I stepped forward.

'Excuse me for interrupting,' I said, 'but I have seen the signore's terrace and it is one of the nicest terraces in Rome. He has dozens of iris and I remember very well the two he has described. As I recall, one was called "Strawberry Shortcake".'

The lady looked at me doubtfully, but the young

man gave me a wink. When the tour was over we all headed towards the gate and I offered my new friend a lift back to Rome in my Morris.

'I'd be delighted,' he replied, 'but you must promise to really see my terrace when you deliver me. Then you can telephone this old battleaxe and tell her what she's missing.'

As soon as we were on our way, my friend told me that his name was Eugene Walter.

'I'm just someone who got loose from Alabama,' he explained with a smile. 'I swam up through the Gulf of Mexico like a lost catfish, and I took a right in the Azores. I do a little bit of everything in Rome. I sing, I play, I write, I dance and I make puppets. What sign are you?'

I told him I was Ariete (the Ram) and he beamed. 'That explains it,' he said. 'There's always a big chunk of the rebel in Ariete, plus you're from Boston, which explains it even more.'

'Explains what?'

'Why we get on. I have trouble with middle-Americans who talk about interest rates, but I get along fine with Bostonians. They are a lot like southerners; they know who they are.'

By the time we had reached his palazzo I knew a lot more about Eugene. He was working as an editorial assistant to Princess Marguerite Caetani, an American heiress and publisher. I gathered his job was not an easy one.

'I have trouble persuading the princess to make up her mind,' he went on. 'She stuffs all the manuscripts she doesn't like between her bed and the wall. If she likes a manuscript, she piles it onto her bedside table and puts a note on it for the author, saying, "Send me something else in a year."'

Eugene's place was a sumptuous building with a balcony on the Corso del Rinascimento and he whisked me up to the top floor in an old-fashioned see-through lift. There, high up on a rooftop, close to the grey dome of the Gesù church, was a flowering terrace alive with colour. The first thing I saw was a great clump of glorious iris in a dozen shimmering rainbow tones. Eugene pointed out the two he had described to the signora and they were even more brilliant than I had imagined. One looked like fine Chinese silk, flecked with spots of lapis lazuli, the other more like combed velvet.

'But, Eugene,' I said, 'you've got the signora beat all hollow. Her iris were full of ruffles and pleats and stripes. Don't you think it's possible to go too far with hybrid iris?'

'Yes,' said Eugene. 'The iris is a stately beauty, but it should never ever be overdone or they look like old whores trying to keep customers with too much mascara and rouge.'

Other spring flowers were ranged around the iris. He had blue and yellow pansies, bright blue forget-me-nots and big clumps of larkspur, which he described as 'the Italian cousin of the sainted delphinium which just won't grow in Italy'. There were rows of hollyhocks, some of them nearly jet black. Next were clumps of dahlias, still unblooming, and two or three bushes of *Choisya ternata* and winter-flowering verbascums.

'And here is my herb garden,' he explained. 'I do a lot of entertaining, so I try to grow the most important seasonings up here. I have a big tub of *basilico*, and another big tub of parsley. If you've got these, you're set for summer. You can chop up the parsley with capers and anchovies and a clove of garlic and you have *salsa verde* which goes with boiled beef. Or you can chop basil and parsley together and add *pignoli* [pine nuts] and olive oil and garlic and you've got *pesto* for spaghetti.

'And here are my other kitchen babies. A big clump of tarragon – and it has to be French tarragon which tastes like anise. Never have any truck with the Russian tarragon they try to sell you in the markets because it tastes like old sneakers. And here are some others – marjoram, sage, thyme, peppermint – I use mint for cooking carrots or for mint juleps. Which reminds me, I have some juleps frosting in my fridge right now.

'I am also growing a little bay tree over there.' He pointed to a tiny plant that had about a dozen shiny green leaves. 'The English call it the bay tree but the Romans called it *Laurus nobilis* and used it to make garlands for the heads of Roman heroes.'

We walked down one flight to reach his apartment, and as he hunted for his doorkeys I noted that there was a little screen set up in the corner right next to the door.

'Oh, that's for Miss Calico,' he said. 'That's where she's going to have her kittens.' I looked behind the screen and there were two little baskets fitted with some nice pieces of flannel. 'She comes up on the elevator,' he went on. 'She is a beautiful tabby, and she is expecting kittens any day now. But she is a strange and biggity street cat, even with me. She is very happy if I bring her meals out in the corridor, but she won't come into the apartment, even to have her kittens. So I have set up a bed for her out here.'

'But you don't mean she comes up on the elevator to see you!' I exclaimed.

'Yes I do,' he said, flashing his best Etruscan smile. 'She used to come up the five flights, floor by floor, or even across the top terrace. But the elevator hadn't been in for more than twenty-four hours when she started using that. And she would never get into the elevator with anybody going to another floor.'

His apartment was as charming as it was eccentric. The walls were covered with a series of large flower paintings, all by lady friends. The first was all petunias, painted in varying shades of blue and violet. On another wall he had an excellent study of sun-flowers. Everything in the living room had a story. There was a big coffee table that he had covered with fake snakeskin, and gold stars had been pasted around the windows and stairways.

'The flat was grimy when I arrived, so I white-washed it all and scattered stars. There is an old expression in Mobile that says, "Some folk are too poor to paint and too proud to whitewash." I just whitewashed it, and it looks fine.'

We went into the kitchen.

'I'm not a chef,' he said. 'I'm just an experimental fellow. I like to make up surprises.' He mentioned an antipasto dish that consisted of an English muffin heated with mustard and hot peanut butter and served with ice-cold bread and butter pickles. A bulletin board on one wall was posted with recipes for an American cookbook he was writing. Below this he had tacked up a hand-written list of 'Advice to Aspiring Southern Cooks'.

1 Try using gin in sauces instead of lemon juice.

2 Never use salted butter. It has a rancid flavor.

3 Never use the dead dust sold as ready-ground pepper. Freshly ground pepper has volatile oils which last only an hour, aids the digestion and stimulates the appetite. Dead dust is dead dust.

4 Avoid prepared mixes. Make it a principle to put back on the shelf anything which has a listed ingredient with a hyphen in it.

5 Don't wash rice. You wash away important nutrients. Pick out the gravel and weevils.

6 Boil baby turnip roots until they are just barely tender. Dress with butter, cream and a flick of nutmeg. A sign of a civilized household.

A series of shelves on the opposite wall was filled with old-fashioned implements such as double boilers, wooden mixing bowls, and iron moulds shaped like ears of corn for making Johnny cake. Stacked here and there on the shelves were odd-looking pink slabs of stone.

'That's red porphyry. It comes from Cleopatra's kitchens,' he explained.

'I beg your pardon?'

Eugene handed me a julep that he had pulled from the icebox. The glasses were frosted and whiffs of crushed mint and bourbon tickled my nose.

'When I first came to Rome,' he said, 'I didn't have any money except from my GI Bill. I was working for the Principessa, of course, but she was so busy she forgot to pay me. A Venetian friend told me he knew of a cheap place up on the top of the Gianiculum Hill. We had to climb three hundred and sixty-five steps to get to this cottage, and all it had was a bedroom, a dining room, a bath and a kitchen with no stove.

'Out front was a terrace covered with gravel and grape-vines. But it looked out over Trastevere and all of Rome and cost about twenty dollars a month, so I took it. There was nothing but weeds all the way up the hill, so I planted some fig trees, which look nice in winter, and all along the steps I planted about a million iris rhizomes.

'While I was digging in the rhizomes I found these most extraordinary pink slabs of red porphyry. Imagine! I knew my sculptor friends would faint dead away.'

'Where did they come from?'

'Well, I know that the hillside was the site of Cleopatra's kitchens. It's in all the books. She had three separate kitchens and she had her slaves cooking the same meals in all of them. Caesar was a very busy man and she never knew when he would be coming home from the Senate for supper. So Cleopatra had one meal ready for him at six, another at eight and the next at ten so he would get a hot meal whenever he arrived. Lucky fellow. I am convinced that those hunks of red porphyry came from those kitchens. Here, take one. Didn't you say that your husband was a sculptor?'

I gave a big slice of the red stone to Robert when he came home from the studio at eight. (Unlike Caesar, Robert always arrived punctually.)

'Where'd you get this?' he asked.

'It comes from Cleopatra's kitchen on the Gianiculum,' I said.

'Oh, I didn't know she was still cooking.'

'Well anyway, when I went to the iris garden on the Appia I met a fellow from Mobile, Alabama.'

'And what kind of a fellow was he?'

'He is a combination of Winnie the Pooh and Huckleberry Finn and he used to live on the Gianiculum in a hut. Now that he is richer, he has a magnificent terrace near the Piazza Venezia. He writes and he cooks, and he pastes gold stars all over his furniture.'

'Doesn't sound like my cup of tea,' Robert said.

When they finally met, Robert and Eugene got along like a house on fire.

CHAPTER ELEVEN

The Late Flowering of Ninfa

WHEN THE HISTORY OF ITALIAN GARDENING IS WRITTEN, it seems likely that the great Caetani garden at Ninfa south of Rome will be named as the garden that marked the beginning of the new style of naturalistic gardening in Italy.

The Second World War dealt a terrible blow to the traditional formal Italian gardens that had flourished for centuries. After the war the old aristocrats found themselves faced with stiff new estate taxes and soaring maintenance costs which left their gardens unkempt and unattended. Public gardens too began to suffer, as local funds were diverted to the re-construction of roads and bridges, towns and cities. Many of the old gardens were eventually abandoned or were ceded to the Italian government in lieu of taxes, and the state proved an indifferent custodian. Among post-war casualties were the Boboli Gardens in Florence, which were so badly reduced that they were closed to the public for extended periods, and the Villa D'Este outside Rome, which shocked visitors with its grimy fountains splashing dirty water (now cleaned).

The great English-made Botanic Gardens in Ventimiglia, called the Villa Hanbury, were acquired by the government after the war, and then left wide open so that vandals could drive in and out lugging away precious plants. (In the end they were saved by the intervention of a group of concerned Italian and English garden-lovers.)

The Caetani, on the other hand, did not feel the economic pinch as strongly as their all-Italian cousins, because the Caetani princes had been marrying foreign heiresses for generations and the family fortunes tended to depend on sources outside Italy. Also, because of the casual, naturalistic style that prevailed at Ninfa, the garden could survive with less trauma than other more labour-intensive places. I was lucky enough to visit Ninfa several times while it was being developed, and I met two of the ladies who were instrumental in making it the lovely spot it is today. One was the Principessa Marguerite Caetani, for whom Eugene worked. The other was her daughter, who preferred to be known simply as Mrs Lelia Caetani Howard.

Their beloved garden of Ninfa, which is located at the foot of the Lepanti Mountains about fifty miles south of Rome, had been in the Caetani family since 1297, when an ancestor, Pope Boniface VIII (a Caetani), bought the property for 200,000 gold florins. To his descendants it must have seemed surprising that he paid so much, for the medieval town was later abandoned, nothing but crumbling churches, tumbling walls and bits of old towers, all covered over by rampant noxious vines. The atmosphere was even

more insalubrious because it was close to the Pontine
marshes, which brought malaria and poverty to the
whole backward area.

For the first six hundred years the Caetani, safe in
their city palaces, had little to do with Ninfa, but
finally in 1890 the head of the clan, Duke Onorato
Caetani, who was considered 'the cleverest man in
Italy', decided to develop some of the family property.
He chose to build a summer house near the town of
Foligno, arguing that the Ninfa area was too unhealthy,
but his English wife, the Duchess Caetani, who was
keen on all kinds of outdoor activities from hunting to
mountain climbing to hot-air ballooning, disagreed
with her husband's choice. She was enchanted by the
melancholy atmosphere of Ninfa dozing in the ruins,
so she fearlessly defied doctor's orders and took their
five children (suitably dosed with quinine) for jolly
picnics among the fallen stones.

The duchess was only one in a line of English and
American women who married into the Caetani
family, and it was probably because of these ladies
with their memories of pretty flower gardens back in
England and America that Ninfa developed so charm-
ingly. The duchess passed on her love of gardens to
her son, Prince Gelasio. During the 1920s Gelasio
drained the noxious Pontine marshes and, while doing
so, found time to nip across to Ninfa to supervise the
restoration of the ruined Palazzo Comunale, turning it
into a summer villa for his family. He also cleared the
undergrowth of ivy and briars from the ruins,
fertilized the roses that his mother had planted, and
gradually began putting in trees such as holm oak,

black walnut and American evergreen magnolia, and a
magnificent row of Italian cypresses that follow the
main street of the abandoned town and give today's
garden its towering green backbone.

After Gelasio died in 1934, the estate became the
summer home of his brother Prince Roffredo Caetani
and his wife Marguerite, and they began the real job of
organizing the planting. They diverted and divided
the Ninfa River that came rushing down from the
Lepanti Mountains so that it would flow through
the garden in streamlets, thus giving Ninfa more
running water daily than many Italian gardens get all
year long. When you add this huge flow of water to
the brilliant Mediterranean sun and the background of
an abandoned medieval village you have a setting
worthy of grand opera.

Eugene knew that I loved modern Italian gardens
and when he mentioned me to his employer, the
Princess, she suggested I come to one of her Sunday
lunches. This was back in May 1961. The Princess
always led her guests on a tour of the garden before
lunch so I had a chance to see it while it was still in
the making. It was all very simple. Instead of the
formality of flower beds and careful borders, Ninfa
was built around gentle walks through nature. Nearly
all of the plants, from the roses to the walnut trees,
were of English origin and the Princess explained in
her marked Boston accent that she had scrupulously
avoided any exotic plants such as palms and aloes and
cycads, which give so many Italian gardens a heavy
North African look.

Her tour led us along the river into a glade of mixed

magnolias underplanted with spring bulbs, and off to one side we would see several Chinese paulownia trees nodding in the breeze and laden with thousands of lavender flowers that looked just like foxgloves. The path then proceeded through an avenue of cypresses that had swoops of white rambler roses twining through their branches.

Roses planted by the English duchess were everywhere; plunging over the walls, clinging to the footbridges and falling into the moving water. There were old roses like 'Maréchal Niel' and 'Alister Stella Gray', and great standing shrubs of Chinese 'Mutabilis' roses covered with pink and yellow flowers.

The Princess led us at a smart pace. She seemed to know every plant in the garden and she would stop now and again to snip off a dead branch or make some comment to a gardener who hovered nearby, ready to take orders. She reminded me of garden ladies I had known in Boston who opened their gardens for charity. Like them she was cool, collected and in command. Coming from Boston I had met many of these awesome matrons who ruled New England society. They had an assured way of speaking that made them appear to have just arrived from a finer, richer planet. Eugene himself, being from Alabama, was disconcerted by the accent too.

When we got back from our walk, several tables had been set up out on the lawns beside the river and Eugene and I were assigned to the one hosted by the Princess's daughter Lelia and her husband, Hubert. To my relief, neither of them had the formidable qualities of her mother. They were both straightforward and unpretentious and you would never have guessed that Lelia was descended from ten generations of proud Italian princes or that Hubert Howard was the son of the Duke of Norfolk. I soon realized that both husband and wife were experienced plantsmen and felt there was much work still to be done on the Ninfa garden.

'Until now,' Hubert told me, 'the garden has been simply a collection of trees and plants. It is an encyclopedia of plants, mostly English. But it has never been woven into an organic whole.'

Steeped in the English tradition, the two were attracted to delicate, suffused colours that created patterns through the gardens, and tried to avoid strong contrasts between one area and another. They came to know all their plantings intimately, and Lelia hated to prune any tree or bush unnecessarily because she liked to preserve the natural contours of every plant. On one occasion, rather than pruning a favourite magnolia that was blocking a path, she ordered her gardeners to move the path to make room for the magnolia.

After the Princess Marguerite died just two years later, in 1963, Lelia and Hubert, who were childless, devoted more and more time to the gardens at Ninfa, and quiet Lelia, who had always lived in her mother's shadow, became their true architect. She did this by painting her garden on a canvas first, and then, when she was happy with her design, she would go out and plant the flowers she had painted.

Lelia reserved her greatest passion at Ninfa for a rock garden built in a corner close to a rural chapel, which she painted as if it was a needlepoint tapestry with each flower carefully depicted. As friends said, 'Lelia knew exactly how much space each flower required, and what colour it should be. In truth she did not plant her gardens, she embroidered them.'

When future historians ask what was the greatest accomplishment of the Caetani family in Italy, the answer may well be their garden at Ninfa. It is visited annually by thousands of admirers from all over the world. The Caetani men built the bones of this natural garden, but it was their women, and especially the last and quietest of them all, Lelia Caetani, who knitted this lovely creation together. She made it personal and gave it a soul.

CHAPTER TWELVE

Unusual Lady Gardeners

THE TREND TOWARDS A MORE PERSONAL, LESS constrained garden style in Italy started with Ninfa, but it has since become almost universal. In fact, after I joined the Garden Club of Rome I became acquainted with a whole series of individualistic lady gardeners who put aside their household worries and went out onto their terraces to throw their energies into growing flowers. Italian lady gardeners, I found, were more exploratory and unconventional in their style, and keener to take chances. Gentlemen gardeners, on the other hand, seemed more traditionalist and restrained.

One member of the Garden Club told me with particular pride that she grew only plants that were members of the salvia family. Another member claimed a specialization in hydrangeas. Another made a wonderful all-green garden in her back yard. And there is one lady gardener, a true eccentric, who spends hours each day digging in her garden right on top of the old Aurelian Wall (built in the first century AD) right next to Rome's railway station.

A gardener who intrigued me from the first was Gabriella Pucci, President of the Legambiente (League for the Environment) in Palermo, Sicily. Gabriella came to Rome from Palermo to give us a talk on the environmental disasters that have overtaken Sicily in the post-war decades. A tiny lady of perhaps forty-two with a smile like a Renaissance madonna, she arrived at our meeting wearing jeans with a jacket and trainers. We realized immediately that Gabriella was not interested in *bella figura* (making a good impression); her passion was *bella Italia*, and her days were spent fighting the property speculators and Mafia chieftains who had already ripped down much that was beautiful in Palermo and cemented over many of its finest gardens.

She first showed us some slides of the disasters that had befallen her city and ended with shots of her own ecological garden. 'We must respect nature wherever we find it,' she said. 'One place to begin is in our own gardens. My rules are simple. No chemicals, lots of composting and a tolerant attitude towards pretty weeds and grasses and small creatures who inhabit gardens. We should encourage nature, not suppress it.'

Not surprisingly, her talk aroused interest, and within a month twenty-two ladies from the Rome club were flying to Palermo to take a closer look at it. As we were circling the airport we looked down on the dramatic outlines of the ancient city. It was wedged like a giant's stage-set between the waters of the southern Mediterranean and the olive-clad hills of the hinterland. In between was a deep valley filled with the vivid green of orchards of orange and lemon

trees. As we got closer we caught glimpses of crumbling pinkish villas and magisterial African palm trees creaking in the sirocco winds.

Gabriella was waiting at the airport to take us on a quick tour of Palermo. Sitting in the front seat of the bus, she wasted no time on the preliminaries.

'What you are seeing all around you is a city destroyed by the Mafia and property speculators. Most of the piazzas and the public buildings were plundered in the "rape of Palermo". Right on this corner was a lovely palazzo three hundred years old. It was there one night and the next morning it was gone. Ugly apartment buildings went up on the land it had been standing on. They bulldozed everywhere, and the people were afraid to say anything about it.'

Now, of course, the city's most beautiful buildings have been sensitively restored.

Gabriella's garden had been part of an old mandarin grove about a thousand metres square, stretching from the terraces of the Pucci villa into the semi-wild countryside around it. Gabriella had heaped it with such an abundance of growing things that it looked like a corner of a tropical jungle.

There were no open green spaces, no mixed borders, no neatly lined paths; a visitor did not walk around with head down looking at the flower beds. The flowers cramming the jungle were mostly soaring through the air at eye level. There were roses everywhere, great swoops of *Rosa banksia* climbing over trellises, and frequently the brick walls were overgrown with climbing nasturtiums. Clouds of the lovely pink trumpet vine grew next to swatches of pale blue plumbago and another favourite twiner, the potato vine, and *Solanum aviculare*, the kangaroo apple, with its purple flowers and bright yellow centres.

At the far end of the garden near a bush of white-flowering pyracanthus Gabriella had organized her compost heap, and beside this she had a pretty little *orto* of lettuces, cabbage and edible herbs. Nearby was a tidy chicken coop, with an assortment of multi-coloured chickens providing free-range eggs for the family.

'These chickens live a long and happy life,' she said, 'and they die of old age. They never go into the Pucci pot.'

One of the final triumphs of the Pucci garden was its hand-dug swamp. 'I decided I wanted a swamp that would attract frogs,' Gabriella recounted. 'We dug this with our own hands. We grow water lilies and water iris, and now we have all kinds of creatures –

dragonflies and crickets and butterflies, frogs, lizards, rabbits and snakes.

'I am especially enchanted with snakes,' said Signora Pucci. 'They climb up my rose bushes and lie there in the sun. I can stand for half an hour just watching them.'

Another lady gardener, Anna Maria Tosini, had a garden perched on a hillside overlooking the sea at Casteldaccia, some miles from the Pucci home. Signora Tosini's garden was her own personal theatre and visitors were warned ahead of time to enter quietly in Indian file and wait in silence for the performance to begin.

Walking into the garden was like entering a greenhouse, for this tiny plot of land, built into a cup-shaped hollow facing the warm sea, was so perfectly protected from cold winds that semi-tropical plants could grow there without danger. A visitor could stand wide-eyed at the gate looking up at the riot of vegetation, for this garden had been deliberately *furnished*. Hanging from the trees were oil paintings of fruit and flowers. A portrait of a lady in a magenta toque smiled down from a rose trellis and next to her was an open pink parasol. Hanging nearby was a chain of big glass balls that added unexpected colour. Rose bushes were swathed in clouds of white tulle.

And then a woman's voice, soft at first but gaining in volume, called out from a thicket of green next to the gazebo:

'This garden is dedicated to my father, who started off as a collector of stones. Some of them were lava stones, dark and sulphur-coloured, and some came from the beach and were smooth as polished marble.'

The voice went on to speak of night in the garden with hungry animals roaring outside, and the slap of the waves on the beach, and then a figure dressed as Pan appeared from the top of the garden and came down the stairs playing a pipe, followed by a little girl with flowers in her hair.

At this point the lady herself, Maria Tosini, emerged from the shrubbery to greet the guests, a handsome woman draped in a costume of pale green velvet. As she stepped down, the fountains suddenly began to splash in the pool behind the summer house, and the guests, some amused, some enchanted, moved forward to meet her.

'I love it,' said a Roman lady. 'She's doing *A Midsummer Night's Dream* just the way she wants to.'

'The play is really not the thing here,' said another guest. 'The thing here is the garden and it speaks for itself.'

Others agreed that the garden, designed by Maria's botanist son, was a miracle of inflorescence. There wasn't a place to walk on the sunny little hillside that was not exploding with colour. Datura trees dripped with hundreds of trumpets; long loops of pink roses twined in and out of the bushes, and mixed with the trumpet vines were the bright pink orchid-like flowers of the bauhinia tree, often known as the Hong Kong orchid. Even where there was no earth left, the Tosinis improvised. On top of the walls and along the steps stood pots of flowering amaryllis and rose geraniums, and old gardening baskets blossomed with clusters of scarlet hibiscus. There were pots of dark red petunias resting nervously on window ledges, and more baskets of Martha Washington geraniums over a metre tall.

One of the minor miracles of the garden was a little alley no wider than a child's bicycle, which looked down on a neighbour's junk-filled space. To camouflage the fearsome nettles and rusty cans the Tosinis had scattered packets of trailing nasturtium seeds, and the nasturtiums had obediently climbed over everything, so that the weedy plot was transformed into a pool of bright orange. On the scrap of wall along the alley, some ingenious Tosini had planted clumps of flowering purple heliotrope that were gradually trained and clipped to form a lavender tapestry against the house. And thus a grim back alley was transformed into a delightful balcony.

If only a modest number of city dwellers would take a tip from the Tosini and Pucci families, Palermo might begin to dream of becoming once again a city of gardens. At least back in Rome there is an ever-growing tendency for lady gardeners to expand their horizons, sometimes in surprising ways.

Until recently all rose gardens tended to look alike, but now there are ladies who grow roses in a novel style.

'A rose is a rose is a rose,' said Gertrude Stein, and she would probably agree that 'a rose garden is a rose garden' because most of the famous rose gardens I have seen in America and Europe are rather dull. The sunken rose garden at the Brooklyn Botanic Garden shows miles of roses en masse; Queen Mary's rose garden in Regent's Park in London is perhaps bigger and more spread out but it looks very similar. Martha Stewart has a rose garden on Long Island . . . If you've seen one you've seen them all. They are built on the theory that roses are delicate creatures subject to savage attacks from bugs and bacteria so they must be placed in a state of perpetual quarantine, cut off from all other flowers in separate beds.

One member of the Garden Club of Rome who plants her roses differently is Maresa del Bufalo. She has thrown away the rule book and created a garden that treats roses like friends and relatives. The del Bufalo rose garden is situated in sunny pasturelands near Ciampino airport, where Roman aqueducts march in broken lines towards the Alban Hills.

The sign over the rose-covered gate tells you that this is 'Valleranello' and the moment Maresa comes to open it you know that it is going to be fun. She is a vivacious blonde, given to wearing Indian kurtas or fishermen's blouses full of pockets; she almost always has a pair of secateurs in her hand and a broad smile. Before showing her roses she generally invites you into her house for tea, and you are struck by the casual informality of the decor and the pictures of her husband and three handsome sons on the piano, along with large portraits of an Indian guru she visits at his ashram in south India.

Visitors tend to nudge each other when they see the guru's portrait.

'Yes, that is my guru,' she says in a matter-of-fact tone. 'I take him roses when I go to visit him every year at Christmas.'

Maresa has little time for idle chatter; she can't wait

to get you out into her garden to see her best roses while the sun is still shining on them. The roses start right outside her front door and the first impression is one of splendid chaos. There are no fences or borders; her flowers just grow naturally in random swirls weaving in and out of a grassy meadow and everywhere you look there is some different colour, some overpowering scent that makes you think of tea or spice or a perfume factory.

It is as if the lady in a surge of excitement danced around her meadow scattering a basketful of newly rooted roses, just as Johnny Appleseed used to scatter apples. She has rambling roses climbing up the trunks of olive trees, noisettes plunging over pergolas and Chinese roses leaping skywards like erupting volcanoes. There is a new dimension here; the garden is not horizontal but strongly vertical like a hanging tapestry from Rajasthan. The grass and the leafy trees provide the background while the foreground glistens with the mirror-like sparkle of flowers.

As one seasoned garden photographer remarked when he first saw Maresa's effort, 'I have always been bored to death with rose gardens. They are prissy and over-pruned. But now I have changed my mind. This is what rose gardens should be all about.' Peter Beales, perhaps the best-known rose grower in England, was so enchanted by Maresa's multi-level garden that he included hers among his thirty-three favourite rose gardens in Europe and America.

Like so many new gardeners, Maresa came to her passion for roses accidentally. In the 1960s, while she was studying landscape architecture at Rome

University, she married an architect and builder, Luciano del Bufalo, who had a two-acre property on the road to Ciampino. The property, with no grass and no flowers and just a few Roman pines growing next to a modest stone house, was totally uninspiring.

'I was certain of one thing,' says Maresa. 'I didn't want any more conifers; they are heavy and full of shadows and I wanted to make a garden that was bursting with sun and colour. So I bought some lighter deciduous trees – winter-flowering magnolias (japonica), and flowering fruit trees, and bushes like cistuses and escallonia.

'I also decided to put in just a few roses, but since I didn't know any names I told the nursery to make up a list for me.' She smiles when she says this because today there is hardly a rose whose name she does not know. It was later on, in the 1970s, that she became more interested in roses and in the next two decades she increased her collection until now, after the Millennium, it numbers well over one thousand varieties.

Maresa is personally involved with each one of her roses. She still remembers where she got each plant, whether it was a cutting or an established bush and precisely how it smells. She also knows the intimate family background of many of them.

I watch while she prunes a thick stalk of her repeat-flowering Frensham roses, and she remarks that it is one of the few red roses she tolerates, because it has a scarlet tint that mixes well with her beloved pinks and yellows.

'This is one of my most vigorous bushes,' she says,

lopping off a branch as thick as a walking stick. 'If I don't cut it back it will take over this part of the garden.' Great chunks of Frensham bite the dust but a smaller bush of the same rose is pruned with more care.

'This is an old lady of nearly thirty,' she says. 'She is the mother of the big boy I just pruned. So even though she is getting tired I try to treat her with more respect.' Another favourite is a musk rose called 'Robin Hood', which is rustic and almost ever-blooming, 'the biggest stallion in the garden'. She explains that by planting 'Robin Hood' next to some of her more timid one-time bloomers she has managed to produce a whole group of new climbing roses that bloom repeatedly. One of her most successful hybrids is a two-tone pink and white rambler named for her husband, Luciano.

Maresa believes that her roses grow so well because the soil is right for them and she avoids any fussy hybrid tea roses that require extra attention. 'I really don't need roses as big as artichokes,' she says.

Her disease treatment is simple: a good dose of Bordeaux mixture in late winter and a combination fungicide in April and again in July. Insects do not seem to bother her healthy roses but she resorts to pyrethrum in March to chase off whiteflies.

Pruning rates very high on her list of chores. She does not leave her garden during rose-pruning time, and when she does travel she carries plastic bags of rose plants and cuttings with her. 'I go to Venice a lot,' she says, 'but there are no good rose nurseries in Venice so I try to make up for that by bringing roses from Rome myself.'

She also carries rose cuttings whenever she goes to India to visit her guru near Bangalore. The Indian customs agents look a little askance when a bouncy Italian blonde shows up with her luggage full of rose bushes. 'I tell them these flowers are not real,' she says, 'so they wave me through with no trouble at all.' As a result her guru is gaining fame as one of the best rose-growers of south India.

While Maresa's roses grow high, a second garden-club member spends her time trying to keep her rose bushes low. This lady is Flavia della Gherardesca. She is introduced to strangers as 'La Contessa della Gherardesca' but she is known to most of the club members as 'Flavia'.

Widowed very young, Flavia has never remarried but has chosen to devote much time to charitable and educational projects. She was for years the Italian president of the League of Women Voters and toured the country encouraging Italian women to take more interest in politics. She is also very active in garden club affairs. Still strikingly handsome with a clear complexion and wonderful white hair, Flavia was an enthusiastic mountain climber and swimmer and even in her mid-eighties she went out regularly with a group of friends to hike energetically in the hills around Rome.

I met Flavia on the garden club trip to Sicily and we got into the habit of sitting together on the bus as we toured from one splendid villa to the next. I was struck by her wide knowledge of Mediterranean trees and flowers. On the last day of the Sicily trip we discovered that we were neighbours in Rome; I lived on the Piazza Borghese and Flavia explained that she had a flat 'very near the Piazza di Spagna, with a nice view'.

A week later she invited me for lunch, and Robert and I climbed the Spanish Steps to discover that my new friend lived on the top floor of a building where the stylist Valentino had several floors of showrooms and offices. We took the lift to Flavia's floor and the door was opened by an Indian butler, who ushered us through a light-filled *salotto* (living room) and onto the terrace.

Flavia's terrace deserved a five-star rating in any Michelin guide. It was a little bigger than a tennis court and it looked straight out at the statue of the Madonna perched on her tall column directly in front of the American Express building. Beyond the Virgin was a wide, sweeping view of the city that resembled a painted backdrop. The hills of Rome emerged along the skyline with the ochre walls of the Quirinale palace to the left and the magnificent cupola of St Peter's in the centre.

Flavia came through the doorway to greet us looking charming in a printed dress. 'Welcome to my terrace,' she said with a smile. 'I wanted you to see it now because this is the best season, and I am trying to discover some new plants to grow here, as long as they are low and bushy. I don't want any tall plants because they would obstruct the view, so I have concentrated on bush roses.'

Her roses were planted in sixty large pots, which she had grouped in congenial clusters on the terrace floor.

One clump included an array of flourishing Meilland roses, which were gathered around a large bush of arborvitae and a flourishing lemon tree. Another group contained varieties of Chinese roses, starting with the vivid yellow and pink of *R. chinensis* 'Mutabilis' and going on to 'Cécile Brünner' and 'Old Blush'; another cluster featured some of the more brilliant tea roses, including the vivid scarlet of 'Lilli Marlene' and the orange of 'General Schablikine'. All of them were in buoyant good health. Flavia said she had so many roses blooming that she cut a bunch every day or two for the dining-room table.

'The only other plant I have permitted myself is lavender. I love the smell,' she continued, 'and I was lucky enough to find one lavender called *Lavandula dentata* which stays very low and blooms almost all year, even in winter.'

We moved closer to inspect the lavenders planted in low containers lining the top of the terrace wall. An original cutting had been divided and replanted dozens of times and now filled some thirty pots, providing a pleasant blue frame for the view of Rome.

'The only thing I do is to keep the lavender trim by cutting back all of the internal stems and twigs when they get dry, leaving only the new green shoots which will flower next. That way we keep the lavender low and it never stops flowering.'

I suggested several other varieties of lavender that might blend in with her planting scheme and offered her some cuttings, including *Lavandula stoecas*, a Spanish lavender with large flowering bracts at the tip of its stalks. As we walked back towards the living

room I asked her about watering all these pots daily;
Flavia said she had never bothered to put in automatic
watering.

'The *portiere* waters them when I'm away,' she said,
'and when I'm here, it is wonderfully relaxing to give
them a little water and enjoy the rooftop life of old
Rome. I often get up soon after dawn so that I can
water when it is cool, and I like to watch the flocks of
geese that fly over at that time. I'm told that they roost
under the bridges of the Tiber and then they fly off to
feed near the sea at Ostia in the early morning.'

We were joined for lunch by her niece, Martina, also
a member of the garden club. Martina greeted us
warmly and then handed a newspaper clipping to her
aunt.

'Here, Zia [auntie],' she said, 'after all these years,
we have proof that the della Gherardescas are not
cannibals after all.'

She saw we looked startled. 'For hundreds of years,'
she explained, 'Italians have believed that one of the
early della Gherardescas was a cannibal. It seems that
Dante wrote in the *Inferno* that back in the thirteenth
century one Count Ugolino della Gherardesca was
imprisoned in Pisa's Clock Tower along with his two
sons, and to avoid starvation he was driven to eat the
flesh of his own children. A terrible story! But perhaps
it is not true, after all.'

She read from the newspaper clipping: '"Now an
Italian archaeologist, Francesco Mallegni of the
University of Pisa, has found five skeletons buried in
a crypt under a church in Pisa, along with a scroll saying they are the bones of the Ugolino clan.

'"Tests show that all five men suffered from malnutrition during the last three months of their lives, indicating that they were poorly fed in prison, but they were killed long before they could starve to death. The count could not have eaten his sons, Mallegni said, because he had no teeth."'

'On that note,' said Flavia with a smile, 'shall we go to table?'

CHAPTER THIRTEEN

Sandra, the Beautiful Cat-catcher

ROME IS NOT A CITY OVERLOADED WITH GOOD SAMARITANS and yet it boasts one sizeable group of cat-loving citizens, referred to as *gattari* (cat-helpers), who can be seen in many of the parks and piazzas of the old city carefully setting out plastic dishes full of food and water for the stray cats. Experts estimate that there are about 150,000 *gatti randagi* (feral cats) in Rome, many of them clustering in such big open spaces as the Forum and the major parks and cemeteries.

The *gattari* are not organized as a group but are a helter-skelter assemblage of cat-feeders – about nine thousand of them women and one thousand men. When they go out on their rounds each day they carry with them a special document from the Carabinieri attesting to the fact that they are official aid-givers and cannot be either arrested or sent away. Since one of their duties is to ensure all the homeless cats are sterilized, the *gattari* are permitted to capture unsterilized cats, take them to the vet, and bring them back to their piazzas afterwards. As their official document supplied by the Ufficio dei Diritti Animali

(Office of Animal Rights) of the Commune of Rome says: 'The work of these volunteers is precious, because it permits us to keep the sanitary and demographic condition of these animals under control. The sterilization of these animals is obligatory. If these cat-protectors have any difficulty capturing the cats who need sterilization, they can ask for help from the police. Keep in mind [the document goes on] that these cats are considered a *bene indisponibile dello stato* [an irreplaceable patrimony of the state] and cannot be removed from their piazza or disturbed in any way.' Actually these words are patently insincere – no doubt they were forced upon the city government by some illustrious animal activist – for, if the truth be known, the Commune of Rome is not at all keen on cats and has almost no facilities to either sterilize or take care of them. In fact if cats have to be captured for one reason or another, it is the Carabinieri who ask for help from the *gattari* and not the other way round.

I had long been trying to interview one of these *gattari* in our neighbourhood. I was aware that one or two older women carrying plastic bags and plastic plates (and often wearing felt slippers) used to visit the Piazza Borghese from time to time, leaving left-over spaghetti or tuna fish for the six or eight cats who lived under or on top of parked cars. But they are no longer as common as they used to be. I asked Giovanni, who supervises car parking in the Piazza Borghese, to ring my bell if any of the *gattari* came round, but he investigated and said the ladies had ceased to visit the piazza.

'I guess the old bags have packed up,' he told me one

evening. 'Most of the cats have packed up too. I hear that the *portieri* are poisoning them all.'

The idea that all the *gattari* were 'old bags' was not correct either. As I continued my search for cat ladies, I discovered that there was one prominent Principessa who lived in a palace on the Via dell'Umiltà and fed the whole stray cat population near the Fontana di Trevi every day. She appeared in the piazza around ten o'clock each morning, accompanied by her maid who was pushing a large shopping cart loaded with special menus for every cat. The Principessa, who generally wore black, unpacked the plates herself every day, and indicated which meal went to which cat. She frequently fed ten to twelve cats in a morning and carried special medicines for cats who needed care. If they were very poorly the maid packed them in a basket and took them to a local vet. The story goes that the lady carried on her daily *gattara* activities without informing her husband the Principe.

I have heard of another cat lady, the wife of a magistrate, who gets up every morning at five to cook a large batch of chicken livers, which she then loads onto a shopping trolley and feeds to several dozen cats all over the neighbourhood. Her husband complains that the house never loses the smell of cooking livers.

What I did not imagine was that even while I was hunting for cat ladies in front of our building, our back alley, the Vicolo di San Biagio, was receiving regular visits from a top cat lady of central Rome, the beauteous Sandra, who came every two days on her motorbike to feed and sympathize with a large black and white cat who dominated life in the alley. We call

the cat the Duke because of his highfalutin tastes – he likes to sleep on the sagging canvas top of our old red Citroën because he finds it softer and cooler than the hard top of even the fanciest BMW.

I discovered Sandra accidentally one morning about eight thirty, when I looked out to check the weather and noticed a stylish young lady drawing up on a very shiny *motoretta*. She parked the bike and immediately was joined by the Duke, who rushed to greet her and rubbed fondly against her ankles while she produced a plastic dish of food and a smaller cup filled with water. While the Duke consumed his breakfast she busied herself cleaning refuse off the street, a gesture intended to counter a common complaint that the *gattari* of Rome left a trail of rubbish behind them.

Then, to my surprise, she extracted more food from her carrier and took it over to a corner of the alley and spread it around among a group of waiting pigeons. As she did this, about a dozen more pigeons flew down to snack. The lady later told me that she fed the pigeons so they would not attack the breakfast she made for the Duke.

Since I was still in my nightgown I could not dash down to the alley, but Gina, who was fully dressed, volunteered to talk to the lady instead. By the time she got downstairs the young lady had disappeared but Gina asked around among the shopkeepers and found a saleslady in a dress shop who had been friendly with the *gattara*. Two days later she produced a card with the lady's telephone number. Upon calling, I discovered that Sandra was not an ordinary *gattara* but one of a small group of specialized volunteers who worked at a private charity called La Colonia Felina di Torre Argentina (the Cat Colony of Torre Argentina). The Torre Argentina square contains the ruins of an ancient Roman forum that has been excavated until it is several metres below street level, and homeless cats have been living there under the arches for many years. Some Romans found the cats romantic, and whimsical poets used to fantasize that they were really the ghosts of Roman senators who had come back as cats to live among the splendours of their past. In cold fact, most of the cats in the colony were suffering from serious illnesses – from FELC (feline leukaemia) to FIV (Feline Immunity Virus), which is related to HIV in humans but is not transferable.

When the Torre Argentina cat rescue centre was organized in 1992 the colony was made up of 197 cats. Now that it is well known, the number of cats abandoned on the colony steps has leaped to 485 a year which means that one or two cats are dumped there nearly every day. The favourite time for abandoning cats (and dogs, too) is just before Romans take off on their carefree summer holidays in July or August.

'It is an uphill fight,' said the colony director, Signora Lequel, who greeted me when I arrived at the centre. 'Most of the cats that are abandoned here are ill and malnourished. Many of them die before we can even treat them. Generally the first thing we do is to try to clean them up and then inoculate against the worst of the cat diseases.

'But more importantly, we sterilize them. That is our priority. The city has a law that all stray cats should be sterilized, but actually the city's veterinary clinics don't work well at all. So we have to pay for the vets ourselves out of contributions. Vets don't give discounts, so it costs us 250,000 lire to sterilize a female cat, and 150,000 to sterilize a male. Otherwise they multiply amazingly fast and all their kittens are doomed to a hopeless fight against disease and starvation.

'Then we offer them for adoption. But the rate of adoptions remains stable at about 250 to 300 a year, while the number of abandoned cats keeps rising. We are slowly losing ground.'

At this point, Sandra, who had been called to a Carabinieri station in Trastevere to give advice about a troublesome tomcat, returned to the centre. She was a handsome girl in her late twenties who looked like a younger, taller Sophia Loren with eyes of a startling green.

Sandra explained to us that she had seen the problem cat in the police station and found him so unruly that it was decided she would return the next day with her cat-catching equipment, so she could take him off for sterilization.

'The captain who looks after the cats says this is a very tough old *maschio* [male] who gets into fights all the time. He's a trouble-maker, and he's sick too. So I've promised to go back tomorrow to capture him.'

Signora Lequel nodded with approval. 'Sandra is our best cat-catcher,' she said to me. 'She understands cat psychology better than most and she studies the animal before she tries to capture it. She has rarely failed.'

I said that I would love to watch Sandra capturing the tom. To my surprise Sandra agreed that I could meet her at the gate of the Carabinieri headquarters next to the Giardino Botanico in Trastevere.

'But you must stay behind me and keep absolutely quiet,' Sandra said. 'It will take two of us, the captain and me, to capture this animal. He must see only the captain, whom he knows. He mustn't see me at all, or hear or smell me. We must keep at least five metres away from him. Do you understand?'

At eight thirty the following morning I took up my position in front of the orange brick gate of the Carabinieri headquarters, which was tucked under the rim of the Gianiculum Hill. Shortly afterwards Sandra appeared on her motorbike. She was wearing a pair of dark slacks and a long-sleeved T-shirt and attached to her bike were two large square metal cages, which fitted one into the other. Strapped next to them was a long-handled fishing net with reinforced straps.

A sentry stepped out to salute her. 'Who do you wish to see?' he asked.

'I'm here to see the captain,' she said, 'about a cat. He called me yesterday.'

The sentry continued to look doubtful so Sandra reached in her pocket and brought out a card which read:

BELLOCCIO

CATTURATORA DI GATTI (cat-catcher)

LA COLONIA FELINA DI TORRE ARGENTINA

The sentry studied the card briefly and then put in a phone call. Within minutes the captain was at the gate – a handsome young man with ink-black hair and wearing a very smart summer uniform.

'I'm glad you could make it,' he said. 'This big male is giving us a lot of trouble.'

Sandra nodded and led us over to her bike, where she proceeded to unstrap the two big cages.

'I don't think we'll use the net,' she said to me. 'That is really for kittens and small cats. A big male cat could easily break it.'

She handed me one of the cages and took the other herself.

'All right, Capitano,' she said. 'You go first. The moment you see the cat you should signal us to stop so he doesn't see us. Then I'll put down the cage and we will hide in the bushes.'

The captain led us past the Carabinieri head-quarters, while some of his colleagues watched our little procession with open mouths.

'Hey, Capitano, where are you going? Fishing? If it's fish you want the Tiber is in the other direction!'

The captain grinned. 'It's not fish we're after, fellows, it's cats.'

Their curiosity aroused, several of the young soldiers asked permission to join us.

'Who's going to catch the cat?' they asked.

'I am,' replied Sandra. 'I am a cat-catcher.'

'Oh la la,' one of the soldiers called, 'you can catch me any time you like, signorina.'

In a moment we had reached the park behind the offices.

'This is the area where we will find him,' the captain said to us in low tones. 'They live here and inside the Botanic Gardens too.'

Sandra surveyed the scene. We were in an open woodland, with patches of sunlight coming through. She pointed to a large clump of yellow broom.

'We'll hide behind this broom,' she told the captain as she handed him the bigger of the two cages, which looked like an oversized mousetrap. 'You should put this cage out there in the open so it doesn't draw attention to us, and leave the cage door open. Then when you find the cat you should entice him to come back here to the cage. Here is a nice piece of meat. Hold this out so that the cat can smell it, and then put it inside the cage. If he goes in, shut the door fast.'

The captain took the piece of meat and nodded doubtfully.

'*In bocca al lupo* [in the mouth of the wolf],' Sandra called, meaning 'good luck'.

'You mean *in bocca al gatto* [in the cat's mouth],' he replied.

The captain put the trap down in the open space in

the wood and went off to find the cat. Shortly afterwards he returned, closely followed by a very large black and white tomcat with half of his right ear bitten off.

The captain walked straight to the cage and put the meat inside it, but the cat did not follow. Instead he prowled around the outside of the cage sniffing the air as he went, until he discovered the open cage door. He studied it for a moment, and then made a decision not to enter. The captain moved up and pushed the meat closer to the door but although the animal put one large paw inside in an attempt to tease the meat out, he refused to go in.

Sandra whispered, 'He's too smart. I'm going to try with the other cage.' She reached for the second cage and quickly detached the bottom section, which was removable, and handed it to me.

'I will try to surprise him,' she said. 'I will pop this cage down on top of him, and the minute I have him pinned down, you must come forward, and we will slide this bottom section under the cage so that he is trapped. Do you understand?'

I nodded, but before I could ask questions Sandra had sprung up and was stealing towards the cat. With the finesse of a champion she slapped the bottomless cage down on top of the animal. The cat let out an angry howl as she had caught the end of his tail under the edge of the trap, but the captain bent down swiftly and shoved the tail inside. Then, while the officer held the trap to the ground, I handed Sandra the cage bottom, which she skilfully slipped under the trap so the howling animal could not escape. She grabbed the trap by its handle and we hurried back to head-quarters, where the assembled soldiers cheered our triumph.

The captain summoned a Carabinieri patrol car. He and Sandra got into the back seat, with Sandra clutch-ing the cat in the trap, and they sped off with sirens shrieking to the vet. The 'Carabinieri cat' had been captured at last.

About two weeks later, I happened to see Sandra when she showed up in the back alley and I went down to talk to her. Her news was mostly positive. The male cat that had caused so much anguish had been returned to his colony a changed animal. A successful sterilization had dampened his testosterone levels, and he no longer got into fights. He had become a model citizen; a perfect mascot for the Carabinieri.

Sandra also had to confront new emergencies. First, there came a call from the Ministry of the Interior, reporting that an abandoned female cat in the family way had strayed into its main building on the Quirinale and given birth to a litter of kittens in one of the air-conditioning tubes. No one knew how the cat had found her way in, but the kittens' anguished cries resounded all over the building.

The indomitable Sandra demanded the assistance of a ministry plumber and located their nest. The mother cat had apparently entered the air-conditioning pipes from an outside vent, and couldn't find her way out again. The plumber managed to enlarge the vent so that Sandra could reach in and touch one of the kittens, but as soon as she felt the fur the mother cat bit her. Sandra withdrew her hand long enough to put on a leather glove, and then pulled the mother cat out first, followed by six tiny, dehydrated kittens. They were taken to the Cat Colony at the Torre Argentina, where the mother was quickly sterilized. The kittens were cleaned up and given proper kitten-sized injections to fight off kitten diseases. They would be sterilized much later.

'We never give a cat out for adoption,' Sandra said, 'until it has been sterilized. That's our first rule.'

Another emergency hit shortly after this – a newly abandoned cat was stuck in a tall pine tree near the borders of the Torre Argentina ruins. This cat had got herself out on the long thin limb of the pine about fifteen metres above the ground and had stayed there crying for more than a day while the cat ladies tried to persuade her to come down. Finally, since they had no ladders tall enough to reach her, they called in the Rome Fire Department for help.

The *pompieri* sent a fire engine with all sirens blaring, and in record time they had hoisted a ladder up to rest on the solid tree trunk. A fireman, dressed in Day-Glo yellow, climbed steadily up the ladder; but in no time the cat had moved out onto an even thinner branch. The fireman reached into his sack and pulled out a folding saw and began to attack the branch, until it snapped and fell to the ground, carrying the cat with it.

'*TRIONFO*,' trumpeted *Il Corriere della Sera* the next morning. 'Rome's brave firemen save stranded cat at Torre Argentina.'

'There was only one thing wrong with that story,'

Sandra said to me. 'They forgot to say that the cat was dead as soon as she hit the ground.'

Just a day in the life, I suppose.

CHAPTER FOURTEEN

Gentlemen Gardeners

AFTER ALL THE BRONZE FOUNDRIES IN ROME CLOSED, Robert started going to the town of Pietrasanta on the Tuscan coast, just above the thriving resort of Viareggio, to have his bronzes cast in the excellent foundries there. If it was good weather, I sometimes drove up with him and we stopped on the way to visit old villages and new gardens.

One recent weekend in early May, we had two projects in mind. Robert wanted to take a swing through the Maritime Alps to visit Volterra, where he hoped to find alabaster to carve. I wanted to see an eleventh-century Augustinian monastery in a nearby town called Venzano, where I had been told that two young Australians had established a flourishing new nursery that specialized in aromatic and medicinal plants.

The alabaster proved easy. We had planned to visit an alabaster mine, but we discovered an alabaster factory in the middle of Volterra where stone-carvers worked in a dust-filled basement, turning out ashtrays and madonnas for tourists. On sale upstairs, Robert found a piece just right for the statue of a little girl he was planning. Alabaster is a splendid medium in which to carve small children, its only drawback being that it is much softer than marble, and must be worked with a file instead of a chisel.

Getting to Venzano to see the monastery was a bit more complicated as the road zigzagged perilously into a lost valley, with breathtaking drops on both sides. But when we finally arrived at the nursery we were greeted by a scene so gentle and sweet that it seemed to have come straight from a poem by Ovid.

Beyond the pale brick monastery walls softened by swirls of honeysuckle and loops of flowering roses, all we could see under pergolas and along the paths were raised beds filled to bursting point with a sea of pinks – rose, madder, carmine and vermilion – along with tiers of violet and pink and purple lavenders and banks of thyme and rosemary, all enlivened by the fluttering wings of butterflies and buzzing bees. A tall slender young man wearing jeans and a large straw hat came up to greet us, introducing himself as Don, the chief gardener. He congratulated us on finding the nursery so easily, and took us straight off to see the flowers.

'I think I can say without boasting that we have the largest collection of sweet-smelling plants outside of England,' he said. 'Where else outside England can you find a garden which contains seventy varieties of pinks, nineteen of lavender, eleven of mint, six of catnip, ten of rosemary, twenty-one of salvia, thirty-seven of thyme and forty-nine of scented pelargoniums, not to mention climbers like jasmine, clematis, honeysuckle and passionflower?'

We wanted to know how he had found his way into this unknown valley. He explained how he, a former geologist, and his associate, a botanical artist, had been visiting Florence ten years ago, and had heard about the old ruin near Volterra. After hunting around, they had found the remains of the monastery and were delighted to discover the property also included a country cottage in habitable shape. They immediately converted the cottage into rental flats. They then set to work ten hours a day with monklike dedication to turn their Vivaio Venzano nursery into the prettiest and most exhaustive collection of aromatic plants to be found anywhere. Gardeners from all over Italy still beat a path to their door.

'You won't find many of those plants that fill full-colour pages in *Vogue* magazine or *House and Garden* here,' Don told us. 'We mainly grow plants for an easy-care garden. No hybrid tea roses here, they tend to get diseases. And no delphiniums or mixed border plants either. We love the little daisy plants that grow in the fields around the house – neat little shrubs with grey or silver leaves that reflect the sun, or succulent plants that carry their own water in their leaves and stems.'

He also favoured many species of roses, particularly the rose bushes that grow in the mountains of China and do so well in the Mediterranean climate, blooming nearly all year long. Bulbs with their own built-in food supply were another favourite, as were rare lilies that grew from seed, like the lovely orange *Lilium henryi* that smells of pepper and the pure white *Lilium martagon*, 'too beautiful to be planted out at all'. Other

lilies he considered easy to grow were those which
had been found by plant collectors in the wild; among
them *Lilium formosanum* from Taiwan, with white
funnel-shaped flowers marked with dots of dark red or
purple on the outside petals, and another Formosan
lily which is pure white. He also grew a Nepalese lily
with pretty pendulous flowers of a greenish yellow
colour, and a Philippine lily, a pure white funnel with
streaks of red on the outside petals.

The gardeners had also put together an imaginative
bundle of iris rhizomes, many of them wild plants
from Portugal and the Balkans. He had found and
grown seven different versions of the famous *Iris
unguicularis* (often known as the Algerian iris) which
blooms with gusto every winter from December to
March. In addition to the well-known Algerian iris in
a deep cobalt blue, he acquired a Greek winter-
flowering iris with white flowers streaked with yellow
in the centre, a Cretan winter iris of lavender colour
and another Greek of purple again streaked with
yellow.

There were offbeat winter-flowering bulbs as well,
including a collection of Lachenalia bulbs from South
Africa, where they are known as Cape cowslips. These
have showy red and yellow flowers borne on terminal
spikes and are grown mainly as pot plants. As he
originated from the southern hemisphere, Don was not
content to let his collection go without a nod to some
of the more exotic flowers from the hotter parts of
the world. These included several varieties of the
dramatic datura plant (now known as Brugmansia)
which must usually be brought indoors in winter. He

was equally enthusiastic about his tropical honey-suckle, *Lonicera hildebrandiana* from Burma, which makes double-sized honeysuckle flowers from June to August that start off a white cream and turn orange as they age. Another sweet-smelling climber is *Jasminum odoratissimum*, which comes from the island of Madeira and has terminal flowers that are a bright yellow and smell hauntingly of orange blossoms. But his favourite was a variety of the *Jasminum sambac*, going by the splendid title of Grand Duke of Tuscany. He first saw this beauty, a rounded double flower with a haunting scent, on the island of Crete, but was unable to buy a plant there. Recently a friend had brought him a cutting that he was still desperately trying to root.

Native plants from Australia were mysteriously absent from the Venzano nursery.

'If you really want to know, it's because I am not all that keen on Australian plants,' Don explained. 'They are awkward and full of spines, and they have no smell. Kangaroo paws, for instance.'

His heart, it became clear, belonged to the patch of sunny hillside in Tuscany where the earth is the true yellowish-brown sienna colour and the swifts dive and swoop at both ends of the long day.

'Venzano has always been a beauty spot,' he said. 'Local people come here for picnics and to attend mass in the chapel. They come to taste the water in the well. Some old people tell us they were conceived here.'

Among his regular customers were Lord Lambton, who came from his villa near Siena, and the head of the Boboli Gardens in Florence, who is trying to rebuild a garden of antique roses in the park.

'The director arrives with a Penelope Hobhouse book under his arm. He orders nineteenth-century roses and lilies by the hundreds,' said Don. 'I think we have the biggest lily collection in Italy.'

After we had filled our car with lilies and Chinese roses, it was suggested we should visit Lord Lambton's villa and garden, which we would be passing in less than an hour.

'It's a famous old Chigi villa from the fifteenth century, and Lord Lambton has done the best restoration job I have seen in all of Tuscany. Many of the new British arrivals don't have the money to spend that the Actons and Sitwells had in pre-war days.'

Don warned us that it was unlikely that we would meet Lord Lambton himself, as he rarely received anyone but close friends. But as we drove south, we looked up his garden at Centinale in our guidebook. The estate had indeed belonged to the Chigi family until 1977. As Don had said, back in the fifteenth century, when the Chigis were simply money-lenders, it was a large square farmhouse with no frills. Its owners took on the habit of enlarging and embellishing the property as their fortunes rose. By the sixteenth century, when they became bankers to popes and kings, the residence had begun to acquire a more stately aspect.

The real *salta di qualità* (leap in quality), however, came in the next century when two members of the family became popes, first Alexander VII who had grown up at Centinale and then his nephew Flavio. Flavio hired the architect Carlo Fontana to design and build an imposing double marble staircase for the west

entrance to Centinale. Fontana then went on to improve it by attaching a graceful arched loggia. This giant step from country casual to papal pomp was completed when marble-workers were commissioned to carve stately ornaments over the new entrances. The west entrance was embellished with the Chigi coat of arms, the papal mitre and the keys to the kingdom of heaven, no less. No visitor could fail to be over-whelmed by all this magnificence.

Fontana also constructed buildings on either side of the southern entrance: on the right was a *limonaia* or lemon house, and on the other a low *fattoria* or farm-house. These new buildings formed, with the villa, an extensive south-facing courtyard, brightened by clipped yews and several enormous statues in marble. Further afield a visitor would find a small chapel, a kitchen garden, an outdoor theatre, a bell tower, a sacred wood, and a hilltop *romitaggio* or hermitage where twelve lonely monks used to meditate. (Their job was to do good works and comfort the dying, in return for which they received books, furniture and food.) Scattered around on this hillside were dozens of statues as well as a series of rustic chapels.

When Lord Lambton arrived in 1977, the villa had not been lived in since 1959. The paths had collapsed and the gardens were totally overgrown with crabgrass and homicidal brambles. But it was a lovely sunny afternoon when Robert and I drove up. We passed through an iron gate and found ourselves in the famous southern court, where the statues of Spring and Summer greeted us along with several swirling green topiary pagodas.

Robert was not impressed by the statues but he was full of admiration for the clipped pagodas, pruned from yew.

'These yews are wonderful!' he exclaimed. 'Whoever made them really knew what he was doing. He was carving a living statue out of a tree.'

A gardener who had been pruning the lemon trees in front of the lemon house took a few steps towards us. He was a tall figure wearing old grey flannels and one of the bright corduroy jackets favoured by Tuscan farmers.

'I'm glad to hear you say that,' the man said in perfect English. 'I prune those yews myself twice a year.'

Robert and I exchanged a glance, speculating in a similar vein as to his identity. Almost at once the man insisted that he would show us the entire garden himself. Nothing pleases a gardener more than showing off his handiwork to a couple of garden nuts.

He led us first to the walled kitchen garden just below the villa. It was built in an L shape that followed the wall of the villa above and had been divided by a central gravel path into ten separate plots, each about the size of a volleyball court. The divisions between the gardens were marked by a series of pergolas, some covered with vines and others with rambling roses.

The first two plots were well-planted kitchen gardens; the next two were given over to flowers. On one side was a collection of flowering salvias, including the deep purple *guaranatica* and the lighter blue *uliginosa*. Next to this was a bed of old-fashioned roses with irises around them, and spaced irregularly among these beds were four more of the big topiary yews.

The next two gardens had large magnolias as their centrepiece. On one the land around the tree was left to grass, while the other concentrated on grey-leaved plants – artemesias, prostrate rosemary, *Lavandula dentata* and a large clump of wisteria.

The garden then turned a corner to lead to four more beds containing rose bushes shaded by handsome kaki (persimmon) trees. In the far corner was an old-fashioned stone cistern which had been used for centuries to collect water for spraying the vines and watering the kitchen garden. This tank had been ingeniously converted into a swimming pool, but by keeping the well-weathered grey stones of the cistern as a frame for the water instead of the usual shining tiles, Lord Lambton had avoided the distressing turquoise gleam of a modern pool.

Out beyond this garden the path led through a clipped rosemary hedge to enter a newly planted orchard where Lambton had set out medlars, quinces, apples and pears as well as a row of lime trees and some flowering shrubs like purple smoke bush and *Buddleia crispa*. These were all growing in an open meadow that was mowed for hay once a year.

As we left the kitchen garden we commented that the new owner had managed to combine, in an ingenious way, some of the best elements of Italian and English garden design.

Our elegant guide shook his head impatiently. 'This is not true,' he said. 'One of the Chigis who lived here at the beginning of the twentieth century had an English mother, a former Miss Elliott, and she laid out this garden herself. Miss Elliott's sister wrote a famous book about Italian gardens, called *An Idle Woman in Italy*. All they did here was to transform it back to her original design.' (I made a mental note that Italian garden histories often contain references to English or American grandmothers.)

Our host then proposed to take us to see the other feature of the garden of which he was especially proud, the restoration of the great seventeenth-century avenue that led from the north side of the villa straight up the hill to the five-storey *romitaggio*. This walled-in grass allée was as wide as the villa itself and proceeded gradually up the hill, ending in two large red-brick gate piers topped by statues. Beyond the piers the avenue narrowed to another gateway decorated with obelisks and balls. A statue of Napoleon stood in one of these nooks (it is believed that Napoleon slept at Centinale) and beyond this was a semi-circular outdoor theatre.

After he had shown us around the woods, the gardener led us down the hill again and invited us into the covered loggia, where he shooed two large gun dogs off the sofa and offered us a drink of superb Centinale white wine. Just as we were about to leave, he handed me a card.

'I have so enjoyed meeting you, madame,' he said. 'And your husband too. You know so much about country gardening, I hope you will come and see us again.'

I thought of calling him several times. But I never did.

Garden restorers really should study the Lambton restoration with care, for he has pioneered the way to the kind of low-maintenance, carefree garden that may still be around when most of the elegant parterres and complex formal plantings of Tuscany have disappeared. As he told us so airily, 'I let the grass turn brown in summer. A bright green lawn looks so out of place in Tuscany, especially in July and August when all the fields are brown.' True indeed.

CHAPTER FIFTEEN

Nature Notes after a Long Summer

IT WAS OUR FAMILY CUSTOM OVER THE YEARS TO MOVE OUT to our country house in Canale as soon as the schools closed and the weather started heating up; but there was one summer when we spent both July and August in Rome. The children were in America, Robert had work to do in the foundry, and I wanted to spend my time in the library doing research for a book on Utopia. Thus we were free to enjoy our Roman terrace – so compact and small-scale compared to our sprawling country garden where we frequently had to scare away stray horses and pigs who came to snack in our vegetable garden, until we found a tractor to plough up the vegetables.

In the city there were fewer emergencies, so one had time to ponder over mini-problems, like why the geraniums were not doing well, where the geckos came from, and why the prettiest vines always tried to escape over the wall onto the terrace next door. Given a whole summer to study such things, we came away with a few tiny new insights into the mysterious world of nature.

For example, I had always been convinced that

when potted geraniums die I have only myself to blame. During our Roman summer, my grief was unmatched as I watched one after another of my prettiest pink geraniums shrivel up and depart. I decided I had neglected them, so I tried extra fertilizer and lots of water in the hope of saving the remainder. But all in vain. Finally, when the fourth beauty began to look peaked, I pulled it out of the pot to see if there was a slug eating at its roots. What did I find? Where the roots should have been, there was a poky little teabag. This, I realized, had been applied by the nurseryman when he first planted the cuttings; it was filled with hormones and vitamins intended to give the plantlet a premature jump-start so that it would produce enough pretty flowers to entice innocent customers like me, while the nurseryman well knew in his black heart that once the plant grew bigger, the root-trap would strangle the flowers. I set to work to cut away the teabag with nail scissors, and am happy to report that two of my half-dead geraniums immediately showed fresh leaves and took on a new lease of life.

Robert and I were also in Rome at the time of the 1999 mid-August solar eclipse. On this occasion, too, our information was on the scanty side. We had long been told that eclipses of the sun caused animals to behave in odd ways. Dogs crawled under sofas and refused to leave home, snakes came in from the fields to be near water, and birds would start roosting at odd hours of the day. At the moment of the eclipse, roosters were also reputed to crow. This gem of wisdom was no good to us because the only rooster nearby lived on the terrace of an antique dealer on the Via della Lupa and crowed constantly at all hours of the day and night – probably from loneliness.

The matter of equipment for the eclipse also had us bewildered. As a child I remember smoking up a piece of glass to view an eclipse, and the idea of buying a special pair of glasses at ten thousand lire just to look at something lasting fifteen minutes struck me as absurd. As a substitute, we were advised to look at the dwindling sun through two over-exposed film transparencies placed back to back.

Television was almost no help to us in tracking this fin-de-siècle sun-blot. About sixty minutes before the great event the RAI, the main Italian TV network, was still running its usual cartoons and cookery shows. Some twenty minutes later, we came upon an unnamed private station that had cleverly plugged into the BBC service from Cornwall, where the eclipse would be at its most visible. The skies in southern England were overcast, but the BBC had sent its cameramen up in a Hercules plane. These shots from above the cloud layer were riveting and, as it turned out, the only decent eclipse pictures of the day.

The RAI, on the other hand, decided to look in on the great event from the top of a mountain north of Bolzano, where a fetching presenter in a miniskirt appeared with a beagle on a lead, announcing that the dog would show us by its odd behaviour just when the eclipse began. The beagle was so overcome by the pretty woman and all the cameramen that it padded around the mountain top exuding charm from every pore, and remained totally oblivious of the great event going on in the skies above.

About this time some of the other stations decided to give the eclipse a twirl, but their efforts mainly involved announcers standing with their microphones in front of hilltop observatories (never inside the observatories) warning the audience not to look up with only sunglasses. Optometrists in white jackets repeated at regular intervals that anyone looking at the eclipse without proper protection could go blind.

We finally gave up on the TV and went out to our wisteria-covered terrace, to discover something the beagle and all the optometrists had neglected to tell us: the eclipse was already well under way in the Rome area. The sky seemed a bit on the dim side so we peered skyward through a bit of exposed film, and there it was – the moon had cut a sizeable chunk out of the western corner of the sun. The apple had been bitten. We took turns with the exposed film watching the moon cutting a larger and larger slice, and as I waited I noticed that the floor of our terrace was covered with tiny pie-shaped pools of light. It seemed odd to me that these twinkles of light, coming through the chinks in the wisteria leaves, were all identical in shape. But the next time I looked up, I realized the little lights on our terrace floor were exactly the same shape as the eclipse itself.

As we studied the spots on the floor, eventually it dawned on us that they were getting thinner and thinner, exactly as the pie in the sky was growing thinner. We were getting some kind of reflection, filtered through the tiny holes between our wisteria leaves. Robert happened to have a camera on hand, so he snapped some pictures. Gradually, as the sun got slimmer, the reflections below took on a sickle shape too. Only when the sun once more escaped from the moon and emerged on the far side did we notice something else: our floor reflections had reversed! As the sun emerged with its arc facing east, the mini

arcs on the floor slowly rotated to face the west. Eureka!

We reasoned, belatedly, that our wisteria leaves, full of very small holes, had acted exactly like the old pin-hole cameras of our grandfathers. Instead of pricking a minuscule hole in a piece of cardboard and placing it between a light bulb and a screen, we had grown a clump of overhead wisteria leaves that acted as a camera between the sun and the floor. In both cases, because of some law of optics, the images had reversed.

Back on the TV screen, the beagle was still charming everyone from RAI. Other shots showed London in sepulchral gloom, while Paris on the contrary seemed bathed in sunlight. We turned off the set and sat watching as the little light bubbles on our terrace floor grew rounder and rounder, wishing we knew more about optics. The sky was returning to normal.

The next day we scoured the newspapers to find out if the eclipse had brought any unusual side-effects, especially among animals. But the only report we found was from England, telling of a man whose carrier pigeons, released during the eclipse, had become totally confused and had returned to home base without any attempt to follow their usual course. American carrier-pigeon experts have long reported, incidentally, that whenever they release pigeons near a powerful radio transmitter, the birds seem similarly confused.

A week or so later we heard from our nature corres-pondent in southern India, a pineapple planter, water dowser and student of 'energy sources' from deep within the earth. He believed that by using the same forked stick employed so successfully to find water underground, he could also locate energy surges from deep underground springs or wells. He had checked out many of the most important temples in the three provinces of south India – Karnataka, Tamil Nadu and Kerala – and invariably found the temples were located right on top of very strong energy surges. He had also found that the biggest trees on his plantation in Moodbidri were on the receiving end of underground currents of energy.

During the last two eclipses he had got up at dawn and raced around to as many temple sites as he could and tested them for the usual energy sources. To his surprise, he found that during both eclipses the energy had been turned off.

'Does this mean the energy you are tracking does not come from within the earth, but from the sun?' I asked him by e-mail.

He replied, 'The cut-off of energy during an eclipse may mean that the sun penetrates the earth and touches off a special source of energy that then moves in a stream to the surface. So it could be that when the sun is covered, the energy stream is cut off.' He had other ideas too, and is still carrying out experiments in Moodbidri.

In any case, having two encyclopedias at arm's reach, I perused the subject over lunch on the terrace. In time I also spotted a few mistaken ideas I had about bulbs too.

I had at that time three kinds of unusual flowering bulbs – crinums, yellow callas and *Amaryllis belladonna* – and they had always performed very poorly for me. Of the nine pots of crinums in our country greenhouse, only four flowered in the early spring. Solution? I read up on crinums, and one dictionary told me (in tiny print) that although these lovely salmon-coloured lilies were famed as shade lovers and their leaves burned in direct sunlight, they also needed a good bit of sun in winter to ensure flowering. I therefore planned to move my crinums to the front row in the greenhouse so that they got winter sun.

Worse yet, I had two pots of rare yellow calla lilies, scrounged from a lady in Quadroni. Although they sent up plenty of pretty spotted leaves in July they gave me no flowers. I finally found an obscure item in the American encyclopedia that said that callas will not flower 'unless all watering is stopped after they flower in August and they are allowed to become dormant for the rest of the summer'. No procreation without estivation. I decided to control the watering of the pots on the Rome terrace more accurately.

The mystery of the non-flowering *Amaryllis belladonna* was solved not by the encyclopedias but by a monthly issue of the Royal Horticultural Society magazine. The Belladonna is known as the

Resurrection Lily, because of its strange habit of sending up nice green leaves in the spring, which then proceed to wither and disappear. The plant seems dead, but it is faking. In late September the stunning pink lilies spring from the earth without any leaves at all, and are the joy of the September garden. I had planted many of these in the main border of my garden in Canale but they never bloomed, while other people I knew were picking armloads of lilies right up to Thanksgiving.

The magazine explained that Belladonna lilies only flower if water is completely withdrawn from them all summer, or specifically from the time the leaves die down until the flower shoots up. To flower, in other words, they needed to sleep all summer, which meant absolutely no water. This explained why friends had such good flowers every year – they grew the lilies in rocky ground and forgot about them for months at a time. Since I had mine in my main border, they got water throughout the dry season and never had the dormancy they needed. This discovery caused me to dig up all the bulbs I could find when their leaves were visible, and bring them to the terrace in Rome. Here, to withdraw water all summer, all I had to do was pull out the dripper for each pot. In September came my delightful Resurrection surprise.

III
CIRCENSES – CIRCUSES

Sports

~

Religion

~

Bureaucracy

~

Politics

Over the centuries, Italy has behaved rather like a pretty woman who has been wooed and conquered by a succession of avaricious and ambitious suitors. In classical times the Roman emperors kept her under control by treating her to bread and circuses. The princes of the Church terrorized her with threats of hell and damnation, Napoleon kept her under his heel with the might of his armies, and Mussolini dominated with parades, promises and patriotic bombast. Finally, at the close of the Second World War, with Mussolini dead and the King in exile, it seemed as if the Italian people would at long last be free to build their own form of democracy.

But it was not to be; even as the first elected Italian parliament was struggling to write a constitution, pressures began to build up from outside. On the one hand, the politicians from the Vatican tried to re-exert control over the souls of the war-worn populace, and on the other, the two countries that had emerged victorious from the war, communist Russia and capitalist America, began campaigning to gain a dominant position in the hearts and minds of the Italian voters. Carloads of money flowed into Italian political coffers from Moscow and Washington, and the Italian politicians, always anxious to please, did as they were told.

A three-way tug of war continued for more than sixty years, creating a shaky equilibrium in Italian politics. But eventually, with the collapse of communism and the steady decline in Vatican influence (especially in regard to family matters like divorce and abortion), the situation altered radically.

The winner in the tug of war appeared to be America, dedicated to headlong financial growth, expanding world markets and hedonistic consumption. The two moral commandments that had gripped ordinary Italians for generations – the left-wing urge for social justice and the Vatican call for Christian obedience – disappeared, yielding to a hard-eyed reverence for material gain (leavened, it was fondly hoped, with a bow to democratic principles and the Bill of Rights).

Television played an important role in this drastic shift because it burst upon a virtually feudal society where nearly half the citizens in the south were functionally illiterate, and where even today only one Italian in eight reads a newspaper. This means that seven citizens out of eight now get all their news and almost all their entertainment from television. The glowing box has become their new altar and the faces on the screen have become their priests, their goddesses, their instructors and their confessors. Television tells Italians who to obey, what to buy, how to keep healthy, and how to improve their sex lives. It also records with glee the endless squabbles among Italian politicians, and has effectively turned the complex Italian political scene into a five-ring circus.

The result is that most Italians today regard politics as something to watch: they have become spectators in the political sideshow rather than participants. They hate politicians and no longer bother to vote.

This dependence upon the god of television has had another negative impact on the country's political development. As things are now organized, rich Italians, if they have political backing, can buy up television stations and use them for political ends. Signor Berlusconi today controls more than 95 per cent of the TV networks; so when his opponents organize protest marches against him, he makes sure that there are no TV cameras on hand to record the event. He prefers to devote his network time to advertisements for dog biscuits or ladies' panties, all of which have helped make him the richest man in Italy.

The searing eye of the camera has also cast a sharp new light on other Italian activities, especially in the fields of sport and religion, until they too have become giant spectacles, watched daily by regiments of quiescent viewers. Perhaps the biggest change has occurred in the soccer world, where television first pumped up the game until it became something close to a national religion. Then, when the audiences boomed to fantastic numbers, the big teams began to sell exclusive broadcasting rights to television stations for mind-boggling sums. Italian teams got rich, players' salaries rocketed. After this, perhaps inevitably, came the crash. Public interest cooled and audiences dwindled; TV sports networks that had been banking on selling more football programmes every year sold less, and started losing money. Soccer clubs teetered on the brink of collapse. The Italian national team, featuring millionaire celebrity players, fell on their faces in the World Cup in the spring of 2002. Everyone blamed TV money for the debacle.

It goes without saying that religion has taken on the circus atmosphere as well. The first religious figure in history to gather one million people in a Roman *piazza has been that most expert of television pontiffs, Pope John Paul II. When he attracted the record-breaking number of young folk to an all-day love-fest on a university campus during the recent Jubilee summer, startled Italian politicians dashed to join him on the podium hoping some of the glory would rub off on them. Only one or two critics dared to point out that while the piazzas were full, the churches were empty and enrolment in the priesthood had dropped to a historic low.*

The much-maligned bureaucracy of Rome has always chosen to remain in the background, but its members run a kind of permanent sideshow on the fringes of the big tent that causes Italians alternately to groan and giggle. Investigative TV reporters comment regularly on the grosser mistakes made by government servants. One network revealed in July 2002 that although there were officially 60,000 handicapped people in the city, the Commune of Rome issued 125,000 special parking permits for the disabled. On the Via del Babuino, everyone marvels at a flashy yellow Ferrari sports car, parked all day every day in a no-parking zone, flaunting a disabled sticker on the windscreen. The driver, young, handsome and able-bodied, was cornered by newsmen but refused to reveal where he had got his permit. Roman crowds always cheer clever men and clowns, even when they are notoriously crooked.

CHAPTER SIXTEEN

A Visit from Betty Friedan

ONE OF THE MOST DEPRESSING SPECTACLES ON ITALIAN television is the gaggle of smirking dancers, dressed in minimal bikinis, who appear on all the quiz shows and cabarets. These are invariably hosted by a plump, balding man who is pushing sixty-five. The girls trip down the stairs to greet this gentleman with shrill cries of joy, and then stand as close to him as possible. They make it clear that they absolutely adore him. The portly presenter embraces as many of the nearly nude sirens as he can, and then turns to give the audience a knowing look. He seems to be saying, 'What can I do? They find me irresistible.' Next, the girls, who can neither sing nor dance, arrange themselves into a ragged line, chests up, and do two steps to the left and two steps to the right, and then perform an energetic bump and grind. After that, to massive applause, they group themselves behind the presenter, each girl jostling for the best position in front of the cameras.

One experienced British critic, commenting on this nightly disaster, was prompted to cry, 'Italy is the land which feminism forgot.'

Actually this is not wholly accurate. For women's liberation did hit Italy with a bang a few years back, and the only reason it is not more widely recognized is because it has, like nearly all Italian movements, broken into a dozen warring factions, so that it cannot present a coherent face to the outside world.

But do not be deceived. For every simpering dancer in her scanty costume, there are three or four bright young ladies in well-cut trouser suits who are now busily editing serious magazines or running businesses. And there are three or four more young ladies, dressed in jeans and padded jackets, who are out there in the bitter dawn sweeping the streets or driving the buses. You might say that feminism has not only arrived in Italy, it has become so accepted in daily life that most people don't think about it much any more.

Things were very different when the founder of women's liberation, Betty Friedan, came to lecture in Rome soon after her book *The Feminine Mystique* became a world-wide bestseller. I was an old friend of Betty's and I was at the lecture. I had known her at Smith College, where I considered that she was the brightest student in the school. She was elected to the Phi Beta Kappa Society in her junior year, a rare occurrence. I was only a B-student myself, but Betty put up with me anyhow.

When I became editor in chief of the Smith College newspaper and began the battle to tear Smith away from its Edwardian moorings, Betty was my most effective assistant editor. After I graduated, Betty became editor in chief, and I was pleased to hear that she gave the Smith administration even more trouble than I had. On leaving college, Betty worked as a contributor for a number of magazines, and she came to visit us several times in Rome. The next time I heard from her, *The Feminine Mystique* had made her famous and she called from New York to tell me about the lecture. I invited her to stay and we arranged to meet at the Eliseo Theatre.

I didn't expect to have any trouble finding her but when I arrived I found the theatre in an uproar. Most of the noise and confusion came from the centre rows in front of the stage, which had been taken over by a large delegation of young female communists, easily identified because of their shredded jeans and low-maintenance haircuts, and several of them were brandishing banners: '*Viva l'Aborto!*' Their noisy protestations had raised the ire of another group on the right side of the theatre. Dressed in stylish tweeds and real pearls – obviously Christian Democrats – these women were holding up hand-lettered signs: '*Aborto è Omicidio*' and '*La Famiglia è Sacra.*'

I was bewildered. Why all this anger, why this militancy? I would have expected women's liberation to have finally united the women of Italy to fight their common enemy – Italian men. At long last they could have participated in a movement that would help transform their second-class status in Italian society. But instead of joining hands and going after their oppressors, they had already divided up and started battling each other. That's Italy. It doesn't matter what the cause is – peace or equality or animal rights – every Italian group has its own agenda. Cooperation is not a strong point.

And what about the real enemy, the men? It had long seemed to me that there was no country in the developed world where women had more justifiable complaints than in Italy. I had heard the same refrain from nearly every one of my married Italian friends. 'I have to get up and prepare his breakfast every morning, and I have to make sure that he has a freshly ironed shirt every day. He drives the Alfa Romeo, I get the left-over Fiat. He has a big bank account in his name only, and I get a piddling allowance once a week. But there never seems to be any extra money. I suspect he's a secret gambler, or he has another woman. When he comes home for lunch, he wants a big cooked meal with pasta, a large main course and then a dessert. If it is hot, he will dump his shirt on the floor to be laundered and go to the *armadio* for a fresh one. If he wants to go out for a night on the town with his friends he doesn't even call me.'

So why were the women squabbling among themselves? I can only speculate that Italians have been brought up for generations with a host of prejudices burned into their consciousness. Florentines are distrustful of Romans, northerners look down upon southerners, and landowners distrust their peasants. People who live in Parioli, in the centre of Rome, look down on the masses who live on the periphery. Communists distrust Christian Democrats. Even Calabrians who once migrated to an unfriendly Milan to find jobs and have now established themselves in the north are accusing the new immigrants from Turkey or Albania of stealing their jobs by taking lower pay. Thus it follows that cooperation between groups is very difficult to achieve. Italians fear that if they cooperate, they will somehow lose their power – and their hard-fought place in the social hierarchy.

At this point in my musing, there was a flurry on the stage and out came three women, the chairperson of the lecture, an elegant Italian hostess in tweeds, an interpreter in a fine Armani suit, and my old friend Betty in a fetching blue caftan. Betty seemed rather bemused by all the noise and confusion in the audience. The chair rose and, after tapping sharply on her bottle of mineral water, proceeded with a little summation of the afternoon's programme in Italian. The hubbub in the audience did not subside. The interpreter then got up to translate the speech into English, but she had uttered only a few sentences before the communist girls began shrieking louder than ever. Some jumped to their feet and started shaking their fists at the Armani-clad interpreter.

'Down with the interpreter, down with the interpreter,' they shouted in unison.

The interpreter looked both hurt and surprised. She was unused to being booed off stages.

The chair stepped forward and tried to calm the waters. 'I don't know what the trouble is,' she said in Italian, using the slightly soft 'r' fashionable in the north. 'This is one of the best interpreters we have in Rome. She appears on radio and television, and she has a certificate to interpret plenary sessions at the United Nations.'

The communist women raised their voices, and some started moving towards the stage in a threatening fashion.

'We won't have her,' one woman screamed in Italian. 'She is right wing, she is from the Christian Democrats. Feminism is not a Christian Democratic movement. The movement was started in Russia by Emma Goldman and we do not want it kidnapped by Fascists from the Italian Right.'

At this point Betty got up and had a few words with the chair. Then she addressed the audience.

'I wish you would all calm down,' she said in her famous Peoria rasp. 'I am told that some of you do not approve of the interpreter who is here today. I did not pick the lady and I have no objection to her. But if you want someone else –' she looked round, a little puzzled – 'I see no reason why she couldn't be substituted.'

This remark, in English, caused the Parioli ladies to leap to their feet, waving their arms.

'No, no, no,' they cried in English. 'Do not substitute the interpreter. She is the best interpreter in Rome.'

This caused a new outburst from the ladies in the

centre, and as the racket picked up volume a lady in the first balcony leaned forward to explain that she was a member of the Radical party, neither left nor right, and such was her admiration for La Friedan that she would be happy to take over as interpreter. Her kind offer was screamed down by both sides.

Betty surveyed this scene of combat, and took to the microphone again.

'I wonder if a person named Joan Marble is in the theatre? She is an old friend of mine. She has lived in Rome for a long time and she knows Italian well . . .'

I began to panic. If there was one thing on earth I was not prepared to do, it was to try to translate the words of my old friend to this audience of screaming banshees. Public speaking was not my thing. But there was no need to worry, as a tidal wave of boos crashed through the theatre – nobody wanted Betty's old friend to do the interpreting. I therefore got to my feet and feebly attempted to make my presence known. No one saw me because half the women in the audience were on their feet too.

As I teetered back and forth I became aware that something else was happening on the speakers' platform. A very pretty blond American was attempting to scramble up onto the stage from the front row. Clutching her caftan, Betty hurried forward and gave her a helping hand, thinking she had been sent by me. Once up and on her feet, the young lady turned, brushed back her lustrous hair and waved cheerfully to the audience.

'If you will just quiet down, ladies,' she said with a marked southern accent, 'I would like to introduce myself. My name is Lucretia Love, I am an American and I am a great believer in women's liberation.' She giggled and went on, 'Even though I don't speak perfect Italian, I would be happy to translate Betty's speech, if you would have me. It's better than spending all afternoon screaming.'

She then translated her little speech into simple Italian. The communists, I suspect, decided to accept Lucretia because she obviously had no axe to grind. She was fun to watch and her unsophisticated Italian made everyone feel superior. (A young American journalist who appeared on Italian talk shows once told me that the producer warned her that if her Italian became too good, she would be replaced. He also advised her that she would get more time on camera if she wore a miniskirt instead of jeans and jacket.)

The Christian Democrat ladies also subsided. Looking at Lucretia, who had a winning smile and was obviously not on an undercover mission from Moscow, would be more fun than listening all afternoon to a gravel-throated American who supported birth control and abortion and wanted to get women out of the kitchen.

The lecture proceeded in a rather disjointed manner with Betty making her way fitfully through her speech, stopping every two or three minutes to toss the ball to Lucretia, who tried bravely but not always successfully to render it in Italian. When it was over, there was a desultory clapping of hands and the ladies went home to report to their husbands that the Americans had made pretty much of a hash of the women's liberation lecture.

As soon as the hall had cleared I hurried forward to find my friend. At the front of the stage I bumped into Lucretia, who was involved in a spirited conversation with a small group of Italians, including several young men whom I had not previously noticed. I broke through for a moment to thank Lucretia for helping out, and to invite her to a small party we were giving for Betty in our apartment in about an hour.

Betty looked grim as I helped her load seven pieces of luggage into a waiting taxi. 'Good God, what a mess,' she growled. 'Those damn women promised me they had an excellent interpreter who knew more about women's lib than anyone else in Italy, and then they led me into that unholy circus. I've never had anything like it before, not even in Tokyo or Nairobi. You know what I need? I need the world's strongest dry martini.'

I had invited a number of our friends to the party, including some Italian journalists who were genuinely involved in the women's movement, and I found to my relief that most of the guests had enjoyed the lecture. Some of the Italian women wanted to know where the pretty interpreter had come from, and both Betty and I insisted that we had never seen her before.

At length Lucretia herself appeared, dressed in a fetching lavender trouser suit, and accompanied by the two young men who had been with her at the theatre.

'I'm so glad I was there and could help out,' she said to Betty. 'I have always been a fighter for women's liberation, ever since I was a little girl back in Carolina.'

She then turned to me with a dazzling smile. 'You know, this lecture did a lot for me too,' she said. 'I came to Rome hoping to get a break in the films, and the two men I'm with said they thought I had real charisma. They are taking me round to Cinecittà in the morning to have a screen test with someone called Tito Brass. He's a director.'

Later I asked one of the journalists if she knew anything about Tito Brass. 'Of course,' she said. 'He directs low-budget soft-porn films, the kind they show on the private TV screens at three o'clock in the morning when the bambini are all asleep.'

The upshot was that Lucretia did get a job with Tito Brass and went on to become a soft-porn starlet in the Italian cinema. The women's liberation movement has a lot to answer for.

CHAPTER SEVENTEEN

How a Game Becomes a Circus

SOMETIMES IN THE SPRING WHEN OUR COMMITMENTS KEEP us in Rome, we like to have Sunday brunch on the terrace. The hum of traffic has disappeared, the calls of workmen are silenced and the city dozes around us in peace and quiet. Most of the citizens have gone to the beach or to a ball game and we enjoy sitting under our wisteria and watching the swifts cutting patterns through the clouds.

But one memorable afternoon a few years back, while we were having brunch with Eugene Walter, we were startled to hear a great roar erupting from our little back piazza. We looked up: all the windows in our building were closed and we realized the noise was coming from the open windows of two apartments across from us in our back alley, the Vicolo di San Biagio.

'It's a soccer game,' Eugene told us. 'They are selling the *calcio* games on pay-TV now, so people who are rich enough to have the equipment invite all their relatives to come and watch. Grandmothers and uncles and children and babes in arms – families watching soccer. It's called the new togetherness.'

From that day on, the football roar became a part of our Sunday-afternoon brunches. To find out whether the home team was winning, all we had to do was listen for the roar. If we didn't hear it, we knew the Rome teams were losing.

But this was in the early days. Television has now turned soccer into a huge commercial circus, and among its many dubious accomplishments is its ability to galvanize very large crowds, not only in the stadiums but also in the streets and piazzas. I felt a sense of foreboding when I turned on my television one evening in June 2001 to watch the jubilant fans of the Roma team celebrating their victory in the 'All Italy' soccer championship, their first in twenty-seven years. They had chosen the vast acres of the Circus Maximus for the event and a crowd of more than a million people, men, women and children, completely filled the enormous arena that the Romans once used for chariot-racing. The multitudes swelled from near the Tiber River all the way across the circus until they almost reached the gates of the Food and Agriculture Organization building – a considerable distance. On one side of the arena some unruly elements had even broken through the gates of the Palatine Hill and climbed up onto the roofs of old Roman ruins in the hope of getting a better view.

The authorities had set up a stage for a rock band and singers, with a long wooden ramp leading into the crowd. The highlight of the evening was to be a 'striptease' by the popular actress Sabrina Ferille, who had promised in a rash moment to shed everything if

her favourite team, Roma, won. I looked out across this seascape of faces and felt a shiver of anxiety – too many people crowded close together with no clear escape routes and no sign of an organized police presence. It was doubly worrying because I knew that only the night before some of the rougher fans of Roma had run berserk down the Via del Corso, throwing cobblestones and smashing shop windows.

I turned off the television and went back to my reading and the next day I learned that the riots I feared had not materialized, although some of the drunks on top of the Palatine ruins had had to be forcibly removed by the Fire Department. Sabrina, the papers said, had appeared on the ramp dressed in a flesh-coloured bikini and surrounded by a bevy of male dancers in tights, who made sure the fans did not get too close. One paper reported that Sabrina 'looked terrified'.

My personal reaction to soccer, evolving from total ignorance to curiosity and finally to disillusionment, reflects, perhaps in burlesque form, the cycle of the sport's progress in Italy. In the beginning all I knew about the game was that it bore a faint resemblance to my old sport, ladies' field hockey. Our team would have a centre forward and two wings on either side, backed by an array of halfbacks, fullbacks and a goalie. There were eleven players in each team, the same as in soccer.

Years ago, when I watched football in black and white, I had a hard time telling the players apart, so I tended to concentrate on the goalies because they wore eccentric outfits and were the only players who could catch the ball with their hands and then kick it or hurl it to safety. To me the most exciting goalie was a rangy young Florentine who looked like Lorenzo de' Medici except that he had square sideburns. His name was Zenga (perhaps they handed out places on an alphabetical basis, and the last one on the list got to be goalie).

When we finally acquired a colour television I learned to tell one player from another, but the event that really galvanized my attention was the World Cup of 1990, held in Italy. The preparations were extravagant. All over Italy thousands of workers put up new stadiums and revamped hotels, restaurants, roads and airports to accommodate the armies of athletes and spectators who would attend. Ground-cover experts were flown in from London to make the grass in the new playing fields as sturdy as the grass at Wimbledon. A lavish new *metropolitana* (tube) station was rushed to completion at the beginning of the Via Cassia north of Rome to help the players get around. The station was opened with a gala banquet, only to be closed right after the games and never used again. A brand new railway line from the airport at Fiumicino into Rome was also constructed, and a smart terminal was built to receive incoming visitors. But people had trouble catching the train at the airport as the ticket window was usually closed and the vending machine broken. Worse yet, visitors discovered that once they got to the terminal with all their bags it was almost impossible to find a taxi. One explanation, never confirmed, was that Roman taxi-drivers deliberately boycotted the new terminal because they preferred to collect passengers at the airport, where they could demand up to 100,000 lire for a simple trip to Rome with an added charge for baggage. The terminal functioned badly for a year and a half and was then quietly converted into an art gallery. It is now being used, I hear, as a hostel for immigrants.

Since the 1990 World Cup was heralded as such a major event, I started paying more attention. The thing I enjoyed most was the audience. Italian spectators have honed audience participation into a dramatic art worthy of the opera, and are almost as active as the players on the field. They stand up and scream, they sit down and sway to the left and then to the right. They join hands and sing, they light torches and they roar, and the noise gets louder and more frightening as the ball gets nearer to the opponents' goal. This thunder is often accompanied by a deep and rhythmic drumming that sounds like a Zulu attack on Blood

River. These may be fairly typical antics from the European soccer crowd, but football matches are also among the few occasions when I have seen large groups of Italians behave with such synchronized discipline.

German fans, I discovered, liked to come to the games bare to the waist or dressed up with clown faces and red noses. Their speciality was to jump up and down in unison. The English, the widely feared *hooligani inglesi*, were not as bad as expected at the 1990 World Cup. But the Italian authorities took no chances and sent all the British players over to Sardinia, where it was assumed that the knife-toting Sardinian *butteri* (cowboys) could take care of them. After they had shipped home about forty-five unruly British fans the Italians had to admit that most of the fights were started by the Sardinians, not the English.

For me, two of the most exciting episodes came during the semi-finals, one between Italy and Argentina and the other between England and Germany. Both matches ended in a *rigore*, where five players from each side take a free kick at the goal from a distance of nine metres, with only a goalie to defend his turf. This is surely the most difficult moment for a goalkeeper as he is under attack from close quarters, challenged not once but five times. The Italian defender in this instance was my hero Zenga of the square-cut sideburns, who put up a gallant fight pacing back and forth like a tiger from one goalpost to the other. One by one his enemies came forward. One by one they swatted the ball, pushing it straight past the airborne Zenga. He had five chances and he missed all of them. The Argentine goalie, Goycoechea, had better luck and stopped two kicks. In no time at all Italy was out of the World Cup while Argentina went on to the final. Zenga collapsed in a heap near his goalposts and did not move for minutes while his teammates dropped to their knees and butted their heads on the grass.

The England–Germany match was something else again. All the lean, keen players from England, anxious to erase their hooligan reputation, played a high-class Marquess of Queensberry game, and every time a German player was knocked down three English players rushed over to pick him up and shake his hand. Nevertheless, despite good manners, the English lost the last *rigore*. Their charming attacker Waddell, who had the last chance to even the score, simply miskicked and his ball zoomed clean over the goalposts. Waddell, considered one of the best players in the game, had to be led off the field in psychic collapse. Afterwards the British cheerfully admitted defeat and their coach smiled as he shook hands with his German counterpart. He was the first (and last) coach in the Cup who did not blame the referee for his defeat. Result, the World Soccer Federation invited the British to come back and play in Europe again after five years of exile.

The final between Argentina and Germany was a far less civil affair. Bad temper and foul play began when the Italian crowd booed loudly through the playing of the Argentine national anthem (because of the rough way the Argentines had played Italy in the semi-finals). Argentina became even rougher during the finishing bout with Germany. The Mexican referee finally called Enough and sent two Argentine players off, while awarding Germany a winning penalty kick. Germany thus became World Cup champions for 1990. Carlos Menem, President of Argentina, did not hesitate to call the referee a cheat.

But a funny thing happened as soon as the Cup had ended. At the Studio Olimpico, the Italian grounds-men, always alert for an opportunity to moonlight, appeared with shovels and began to dig up the special grass grown on the soccer pitch, roots and all, cutting it into five-centimetre squares and wrapping them in special plastic packets. These packets were then sold to all comers as souvenirs at 10,000 lire apiece. Even at ground level, soccer had never been just a game.

This commercial development had much to do with television money. In the early days the networks used to cover the big soccer matches and show them to the public free. Then soccer clubs began charging the net-works for exclusive rights to cover the games, and the networks in turn started to make the public pay to watch. The clubs got richer, and the networks grew more ambitious.

This commercialization was already well advanced in 1990 but things have become really outrageous since then. As the *Observer* wrote in May 2000, 'For the past ten years right across the continent, every time a contract for exclusive rights to televise football was renegotiated, the price rose sharply, in some cases exponentially. The pattern was apparently limitless, to such an extent that one club chairman described tele-vised football as "a licence to print money".' The

Observer added that in the 2001/02 season, the combined value of TV contracts covering Europe's biggest leagues was a 'staggering £1,794 million'. As these sums rise, television money has become the chief supporter of most of the teams of Europe.

With the clubs making such a huge income the competition for star players took off too, and within a decade transfer fees for players rose by a stunning 340 per cent. In 1996, transfers for top players averaged between £15 and £16 million a player, a phenomenal amount at the time. Five years later, fees for players had doubled.

The players have got the message too and demand ever bigger sums. Right after the 1990 Cup, one of England's best players, Alan Hansen, was earning £3,000 a week. The stars on the soccer circuit are multi-millionaires now and the gossip columnists treat them like Hollywood celebrities. They drive Ferraris, hire bodyguards and investment counsellors, and many of them have married the kind of TV starlets and toothsome models who previously spurned footballers for racing drivers or tennis champions.

But now dark clouds loom on the horizon. Many Italian clubs have been living too well for too long and suddenly they find that the pot that paid for this extravaganza – television money – is shrinking, not growing. The reason is simple. People still love soccer but they are not ready to pay limitless sums to watch second- and third-rate games. The enthusiasm for pay-per-view or PPV soccer is waning fast. Some people say PPV stands for 'Pretty Poor Value'. Italian broadcasters who signed lavish four-year deals with the clubs in 1999, in the expectation that they would make billions when the football-mad public rushed to buy their programmes, found that in reality the public was not all that keen. These broadcasters are close to collapse. The fans love to follow the best games and best players but, as the *Observer* said, 'Trying to sell sport that isn't top-drawer for top-drawer prices just isn't on.'

An additional problem in Italy is that an estimated two million fans managed to acquire cheap pirated versions of the smart cards needed to access the PPV channels, so they are now watching all the games for free. The near-collapse of TV suppliers has had a devastating effect on major Italian clubs that in the 2001 season were already heavily in the red. Even old clubs like Roma and Lazio were spending more than 100 per cent of their income on the players and sometimes failed to come up with their salaries. The once-prosperous Fiorentina team was facing bankruptcy. Club owners started extending their seasons so that they had more games to sell to the public, and they insisted upon stellar performances from their stars. The stars in turn became more injury-prone. They were tired.

In the months leading up to the World Cup of 2002 the Italian sports press tried to downplay the bad news. The theory was that the matches would rekindle public enthusiasm. There was also the fond hope that if Italy won the World Cup, Italian soccer would sail into happier waters.

Since the Cup was being held for the first time in the Orient, where prestige is important, Japan and South

Korea outbid each other in an effort to build the most expensive state-of-the-art stadiums in the world. Japan spent four billion dollars while South Korea spent a mere two billion, each on ten new stadiums. One arena in Sapporo, Japan, had a grass pitch that could be raised by ten centimetres with compressed air and rolled into the stadium ready for play. Many experts claimed that the two countries would be bankrupt just on the luxurious construction of arenas. A Japanese writer pointed out that since soccer was still a new and unfamiliar sport in Asia, 'there is no way these grandstands will ever be filled again'. But the stadiums weren't the only extravagance on the World Cup scene. The whole event was pumped up by the media and merchandizers, who called it the biggest single sporting event on the planet. The football championship had become a global media circus.

In the old days, when the national teams were departing for the World Cup, there were pictures of the players carrying their suitcases onto local buses to be taken to the airport. In 2002 the departure for Asia was a de luxe affair. The millionaire captain of the British team, David Beckham, and his ex-Spice Girl wife threw a glittering party on their estate to say goodbye to friends. The Beckhams did not pay for this affair. Sports advertisers and celebrity magazines picked up the tab in return for exclusive rights to film the party. Subsequently the British team rolled out to Heathrow in limousines to take a specially chartered plane to Dubai, where the players and their kin were given a pre-game session of rest and relaxation in one of the world's most exclusive resort hotels.

The Italian team skipped Dubai but the players were given a rousing send-off in Rome by both President Ciampi and Prime Minister Berlusconi. The players flew eastward with retinues that would do justice to an American president or even the Pope himself. A key Italian attacker, Totti, was accompanied by his brother, his niece Giulia, a brother-in-law and his fiancée. It was reported that some players travelled with not only their managers but also their personal financial advisers.

Back home, Italy virtually went on strike for the duration of the Cup. To its credit the television network RAI had purchased the rights to broadcast the matches, so the Italian public was able to see all the major games free of charge. They watched from their homes, their clubs and also their factories, where giant screens were set up right on the workplace floor. It was alleged that because of the importance of television money, the games were often played at night in Asia just so they could be shown live in Europe around lunchtime.

When the Italian team's first game began, the streets of the nation were deserted and the RAI reported that nine out of every ten Italians hunkered down to watch. In the opening contest against Ecuador, neither side played well but the Italians won without much trouble.

During the second match, against Croatia, which the Italians were supposed to win, a Danish line judge disallowed not one but two of the Italian goals, and the Italians were declared the losers. The sense of shock and disbelief was felt from the Dolomites in the north to the southern tip of Sicily. In the press, on the tube and in the streets, Italians agreed they had been robbed. Some sports writers began to murmur about a conspiracy, hinting that the head of the soccer federation had persuaded the referees to treat Italy with extra severity. The idea was that South Korea, co-host of the games and builder of glorious stadiums, should get special treatment.

But one or two columnists had other thoughts. 'The Italians are playing very badly,' wrote a Milanese observer. 'They are *uomini bolliti* [boiled men].' The Italians were not the only sufferers. Two other teams favoured to win the Cup – France and Argentina – were eliminated without reaching the second round. France was kicked out by an obscure team from Denmark; Argentina, which had done poorly in its initial matches, was unable to do better than tie with Sweden and was thus eliminated. Pictures in the papers showed the Argentine millionaire ace Batistuta heading for the airport, looking like a man who had been bashed on the head with a shovel.

What was going wrong for the major teams? Too much money seemed to be the most common answer. 'These superstars from Europe are getting too rich. They aren't paying attention to soccer any more, they're giving parties and counting up their wealth,' said some.

Italy was given another chance to go through in its match with Mexico. When play was nearly over Mexico was leading 1–0, and it looked as if Italy would be sent home along with Argentina and France. But at the very last minute, a substitute player, Alex del Piero, was sent onto the field to try his luck. Miraculously, he managed to catch a flying ball with his forehead and deliver it smartly into the goal. The score – 1–1 – provided the crucial point Italy needed to qualify. This was the only happy moment the Italians had during the entire Cup.

After Italy lost to South Korea, there was more outrage: 'Italy has lost in a *Mondiale Sporco* [Dirty World Cup],' trumpeted the austere Milanese daily *Corriere della Sera*. 'We were robbed by a conspiracy of referees,' screamed the columnists. Even the Italian President, who measures his words, announced, 'We deserved to win.'

Only a few of the foreign sports writers dared to express a contrary opinion. Rob Hughes, the dean of US soccer writers, charged that the Italians were poor sports who 'did not accept defeat in the proper manner'. *New York Times* writer George Vecsey wrote:

Europe brought this disgrace upon itself by expanding the season to fill the great maw of cable networks around the world. They had mid-week cup games all season long, and championship games stretching into May.

Want to know why Zidane and Maldini and Figo all looked like they were running into quicksand this month? Because the European leagues and owners are greedy. We do not hear Silvio Berlusconi [who owns AC Milan] blaming himself because his captain, Maldini, has aged in dog years. It's more money in the cable bank for Berlusconi.

There is your conspiracy, sporting friends. European

soccer leaders have made money from the dead legs, dead brains and dead national teams.

Now the Italians are facing the music. First they whipped up the sport into a circus with endless play and endless profits, and now, as the rich but tired players come home in defeat, they are seeing their whole world collapse. The great Fiorentina team of yesterday did indeed go bankrupt after the 2002 Cup, and it is believed that others will follow. Average players are being fired, good players are taking salary cuts. Other stars have even volunteered for a reduction in pay. Club owners are talking of salary caps. People who love the game say that Italian football will never be the same again.

'We are all spoilt,' said one coach. 'What we must do now is stop spending money on foreign stars, and go out to the junior clubs to see how the kids are playing. They are the ones who really love the game. Every *ragazzino* in Italy grows up kicking a soccer ball down the street. These kids could be the ones to turn this circus back into a sport again.'

CHAPTER EIGHTEEN

Our Borghese Pope

From the deathbed speech of Pope Nicholas V, 1455:
We want your graces to know and to understand that
there were two main reasons for our buildings. Only
those who come to understand the Church's origin and
growth from their knowledge of letters realize that the
authority of the Roman Church is the greatest and
highest. The throngs of all other peoples, ignorant of
letters and wholly untouched by them, lose their belief
in the course of time ... unless they are moved by
certain extraordinary sights.

THE NEED FOR POMP AND DISPLAY HAS BEEN A CONSTANT
preoccupation of the Catholic Church throughout
its history. We see this still in the huge public celebra-
tions and the 'extraordinary sights' that feature in the
travels of Pope John Paul II and his entourage. It
remains for history to decide how important these
turnouts – lavishly reported by television – have been
to the Church's history.

I have recently become interested in another pope
who attempted to ensure his place in history not by

travelling but by building 'great buildings' to impress the humble multitudes. This gentleman, before he became pope in 1605, was known as Cardinal Camillo Borghese, and he owned our palace on the Piazza Borghese, where he probably lived for a number of years before his election. The famous Tempesta map of 1592 shows our palace sitting prominently on one side of the piazza with a large banner flying jauntily from the *altana* on the roof, an indication that its owner, Cardinal Borghese, was in residence.

For many years we never dreamed that we were living in anything as grand as a genuine cardinalitial palace, but a friend who lectures on Renaissance art discovered that our building was put up specially to house 'a prince of the church'. Cardinals' palaces, she told us, always feature an imposing balcony above a main door so that His Eminence could make regular appearances on holy days to bless the multitudes. (Mussolini, taking a chapter from the Vatican's book, liked to speak from balconies too.)

Our building's other distinguishing feature is a large entrance at street level, wide enough for a cardinal's coach to enter. Just opposite it, inside the building, there is an ample marble staircase that the cardinal and his entourage could have used to reach the noble reception halls on the first floor. Higher up, on the less noble third and fourth floors where our apartment is located, there were more rooms for dependants of the cardinal, including poets, musicians and scholars, and on the very top (cold in winter and hot in summer) there were relatively cramped dormitories for the household servants, who would have had to run up and down peripheral staircases to serve their masters.

We are told our palazzo may have been a perfect way-station in Camillo Borghese's climb to the papacy, a role that would make him not only Bishop of Rome but also head of Christendom and ruler of the Papal States. For while he was busily decorating our palazzo on one side of the piazza, he was already building a far more ambitious and elegant residence on an opposite corner, destined to become the great Palazzo Borghese. This building completely dwarfed our little palazzo but was totally suitable for a man who aspired to be pope.

The big Palazzo Borghese is even today the most important building in our part of central Rome. It houses illustrious tenants: an eccentric Borghese prince or two; the Embassy of Spain; Checci Gori, the former owner of the bankrupt Fiorentina soccer club, and the headquarters of the most aristocratic social club in the city, Il Circolo della Caccia (the hunt club), where only those with blue blood in their veins can dream of becoming members.

The cardinal gave much importance to his great palazzo, and the moment he became Pope Paul V in 1605 he threw all his energy into speeding up the building work so he could move his extended family into it. Among the relatives whom he brought from Siena to Rome were his brother with his wife and son, and his sister with her husband and a son named Scipione Caraffelli. On Paul's orders, Scipione changed his name from Caraffelli to Borghese and within three months he was elevated to the position of cardinal at the Holy See, where he quickly gained

political, ecclesiastical and financial benefits. During
his first year in the purple Scipione's income grew
from 108,000 scudi to 189,000. One of the quickest
and surest ways to achieve fame and fortune in those
days was to have a favourite uncle who became pope.
The name of the game was nepotism.

It may have been a slight problem of accreditation
that caused Paul to transfer at least six members of his
family from Siena to Rome as quickly as possible, for
although he was born in Rome he had been brought up
in Siena. By moving his family to a swanky new
palazzo in the capital he hoped to transform himself
instantly into a born-and-bred Roman pope, brimming
with good will towards his native city. His manoeuvre
paid off. By the end of his reign Paul had established
a reputation as one of the great benefactors of the city,
and at the same time he had made the Borgheses of
Rome, a rather modest family, as rich and important as
the Colonnas or the Orsinis.

How did he explain his contradictory roles as family
enricher and civic benefactor? The answer is that Paul
didn't stoop to explain anything, he simply embellished his record as he went along. Like other popes
before him who were among the first spin doctors of
history, he used the media available to him – coins,
pamphlets, broadsides and particularly papal medals
– to boast of his civic benevolence. In the goodly
number of medals struck during his nineteen-year
reign, we can see how he burnished his image by con-
centrating solely on his most important contributions
to the public good, or, as the song goes, by accentuating
the positive and eliminating the negative.

Paul's medals (on display at the British Museum) usually show his head in profile with a rendering of his good works on the obverse side. The profile indicates a robust and handsome man with a determined jaw made more determined by a sharply pointed beard. In most of the medals the Pope is posing as the Bishop of Rome in an embroidered cape, but in several where he is celebrating his best work he tries to play down the notion of splendour by wearing only a simple monk's robe and cap.

Only when I started looking into the life and fortunes of Paul (as they appear in medals) did I realize that he was a man in an unseemly hurry. In the very first weeks of his long reign, he was already pushing his builders to finish work on the Palazzo Borghese. At the same time he ordered the reconstruction of a number of public buildings, from St Peter's to the Vatican, the Quirinale palace and the Basilica of Santa Maria Maggiore. As he rode in triumph to receive his papal tiara, it could be said that he carried under one arm a great roll of architectural blueprints designed to change the face of Rome itself and, not incidentally, to boost the economic and social position of the Borgheses.

The Palazzo Borghese was first on his list, but St Peter's came a close second. In the very first month of his papacy, he set up a commission to decide how to complete the reconstruction of the new St Peter's Cathedral, which had been dragging along in an unfinished state for the better part of a hundred years. Squabbling popes and architects had agreed that the old Christian basilica had to go but they couldn't come to any firm decision about how to construct the new church. In 1504, Pope Julius had tried to move things forward by bringing in Bramante, who tore down the original and started rebuilding. In my opinion Bramante's plan, shown in a Julian medal of 1506 and involving a large clock tower on either side of the dome, was far more graceful and less austere than the eventual design. But Bramante's work sputtered along for years less than half finished. In 1546 Pope Paul III, anxious to complete the job, commissioned Michelangelo to provide a plan of the finished building. Michelangelo radically changed the earlier design and declared that the new dome and the façade should be based on the Pantheon and not upon Bramante's drawings. Unfortunately Michelangelo died in 1564, leaving St Peter's still half finished and domeless.

By the time Paul V came to the throne there was a whole generation of Romans who had never seen St Peter's with any roof at all. Only thirty days after he had been elected, Paul appointed a committee of cardinals to make the final decisions on the shape of the new building, especially the façade. But the cardinals couldn't make up their minds, so Paul took the decision himself. He ordered work to begin immediately on a new façade based on Michelangelo's design. A year later he issued the first medal to celebrate the new St Peter's with its dome and façade in place. The startled cardinals realized that Paul had jumped the gun; in the end, to save themselves from making a *brutta figura*, they accepted the new church built to Michelangelo's specifications.

To be sure of being remembered for his decision Paul ordered an ostentatious dedication to be carved in large gold letters across the new façade: PAULUS BORGHESIS ROMANUS. By inscribing his own name in capital letters on the new building just as the Roman emperors used to do, and emphasizing his Roman credentials, Paul seemed to be claiming sole credit for St Peter's, while in truth it took a hundred years and thousands of builders, architects and churchmen to get the job done.

But St Peter's was only the first and most visible of Paul's building projects. On 25 June 1605, just twenty-one days after his arrival in the Vatican, he was also making plans to build and elaborate his own burial chapel in the great church of Santa Maria Maggiore in the centre of Rome. Heedful of the uncertainties of life, Paul was in a rush to get the chapel constructed. His architects' plans were ready in August 1605, and he personally placed the foundation stone and issued a medal towards the end of the same year which showed an early version of his Pauline Chapel, based closely upon the neighbouring chapel built by Sixtus. In the next two years he issued two more medals showing work in progress on the chapel. Both medals feature builders and stonemasons scrambling up the walls of the new building.

A third building project that Paul V found time to tackle, only thirty-seven days after his coronation, concerned the Quirinale palace, perched on the airy Quirinale Hill with lovely gardens and a prime view of Rome. Many of the popes, including Paul himself, preferred to spend summers in the Quirinale because it was much breezier than the low-lying Vatican, which was near the Tiber and tended to be both hot and buggy.

Before its improvement the Quirinale had been a pleasant country villa, but it needed to be vastly enlarged and made more comfortable in winter before it could provide the splendour that Paul and his nephew Cardinal Scipione Borghese required. The improvements that the two initiated more than doubled the size of the building, and made it probably the largest and most elegant of all of the great Roman palaces. Scipione's grand balls in the new ballroom were the talk of Roman society.

The building ambitions of Pope Paul V were not unusual among Italians of wealth and power. His namesake Pope Paul IV, elected in 1593, was depicted in a fresco by Vasari busily vetting blueprints for all his palatial projects. And a present-day Italian grandee, Prime Minister Berlusconi, first elected in 1994, adheres to the same tradition by spending millions on luxury properties in Rome, Milan, Sardinia and Bermuda. Probably his favourite villa is at Arcore, near Milan, where he has also built his own pharaonic tomb. As for good deeds, Berlusconi has recently unveiled plans to build the world's longest bridge. It will link mainland Italy with a reluctant Sicily, where water is now so scarce the people have taken to the streets to protest. The Sicilians claim that they need water far more than they need a bridge to Calabria.

This Italian water shortage is nothing new. In fact Pope Paul V was well aware during his reign that the Vatican, the Borgo and Trastevere all suffered from serious shortage. To remedy the situation, he rebuilt an aqueduct to increase the supply. With his usual dispatch Paul purchased from Virgilio Orsini (for 25,000 scudi) the rights to the springs near Lake Bracciano, north of Rome. His architects then embarked on a project to restore the aqueduct that had been built under the Emperor Trajan – although Paul changed its name from Acqua Traiana to Acqua Paola.

His first medal in 1609 celebrating this event shows the usual profile of Paul, this time wearing the garb of a simple friar, to stress his saintliness, and on the obverse side there is a picture of the Acqua Paola traversing the countryside from Bracciano to the Porta di Pancrazio on the Gianicolo, where the Acqua Paola fountain still stands two storeys high and looking more like a ceremonial gate than a fountain. Only the great torrents of water pouring from three taps at its base reveal its true purpose.

There is no doubt that this new source of water gushing into Rome brought considerable relief to the people of Trastevere and the Borgo, but its main beneficiary was probably the Vatican itself. Once the

Acqua Paola project was complete, Paul commissioned his architect, Carlo Maderno, to build three new fountains in the Vatican gardens that would use the new supply. He also had built in the centre of St Peter's Square another fountain that sends a great stream from Acqua Paola into its basin for all the world to see.

The Pope's venture into aqueduct-building was later to cause acrimony between the Vatican and the Commune of Rome, because Paul claimed that since the project was beneficial to Rome the city should help pick up the tab. Paul had contributed 400,000 scudi out of Vatican funds for the operation, and he wanted the city to contribute as well. After a certain amount of grumbling, the city did in fact pay up. Records show that in addition to bringing water to the Vatican gardens, Paul made plans for a water-mill using Acqua Paola, which would have generated income for the papacy and also perhaps for the Borghese family itself. But this venture was never completed. Even the most generous of public benefactors must be careful, now and again, not to appear to be making personal profit at public expense.

Paul's foresight in bringing a better water supply into Rome is to be praised. I can think of no other European city where fountains, big and small, bring such a constant supply of water to the thirsty citizens. In our neighbourhood, for instance, there is a large fountain in the central courtyard of the Palazzo Borghese and from the time of the Renaissance the generous owners have permitted local residents to come there to wash their clothes, rinse their bottles and even soap down their children. This water, Acqua Vergine, is one of the sweetest drinking waters of Rome. It enters Rome near the Roma Termini, and winds its way across to the Trevi Fountain, a triumphant union of water and architecture. From there the Acqua Vergine moves on to the Barcaccia (old boat) Fountain by Bernini in the Piazza di Spagna, built in memory of the great Tiber flood of 1598 (when boats like this were used to bring food to Romans stranded on rooftops). Eventually this water travels down Via Condotti (water conduit) until it emerges at the Palazzo Borghese and then goes on to a small fountain in the outdoor market just behind the palazzo, where greengrocers can always get water to freshen up their spinach or salad and rinse their artichokes.

Only a short distance down the street this Acqua Vergine reaches the basement of our building at Piazza Borghese 91, where a great tank of running water was available to the inhabitants for washing. (There is a sign right next to our front door showing the level of the Acqua Vergine water pipe.) In this gloomy sub-terranean *vasca* (tank) the laundresses would pile their linen in baskets on their heads, and then carry it up four storeys to the *altana*, a roof terrace. Instead of clothespegs, they used to tie down their clothes with neat little white strings that were permanently fixed to the clothes line. This tradition of drying clothes on the roof was still maintained when we moved in; and every family was given the key to the roof once a week.

This arrangement finally ceased about five years ago when our landlord, La Cattolica, redecorated the top floor and turned it into a luxury apartment, and connected it with a spiral staircase to our drying roof on top. The new tenants of this spacious duplex soon filled the top terrace with a sky garden complete with a grape arbour, roses and old olive trees, so we had to go elsewhere to do our drying. Now, time having marched on, we have bought a dryer.

As the contented residents of one of Paul's buildings, Robert and I have reason to appreciate our ex-landlord's taste. Our palazzo is serene and comfortable even today and we would much prefer to live here than in the great monster across the piazza.

In either palazzo, big or little, we would have the advantage of living in the centre of Rome. We are only about five minutes from the Piazza di Spagna with a chance to shop in the stylish Via Condotti on the way, and in the other direction we have a ten-minute walk down the Lungotevere to reach the Vatican across the Ponte Sant'Angelo. We are also fortunate to have a good outdoor market just behind the Palazzo Borghese, where we can buy fresh fruits and vegetables every day.

The big Borghese palace has some built-in problems. The Circolo della Caccia, for instance, is constantly having receptions of one sort or another, and these tend to fill up the inner courtyard and the piazza with luxury cars that park illegally and deprive residents of their spaces. Also, as I mentioned earlier, the Spanish Embassy, which would appear to be a peaceful spot, is frequently under threat of attack from dissident Basques. One night when the children were still young we were all awakened by a terrifying explosion, which threw me out of bed. At first all we could hear was glass breaking all around us; the noise seemed to come from the tax office across the street, but then we heard a wail of sirens from the Piazza Borghese. Robert flung himself into trousers and shirt and went out bravely to see what was up. He found that Basque separatists had dynamited the entrance to the Palazzo Borghese and the door, a huge fixture of solid chestnut more than ten feet high, had been blown off its hinges. The door was replaced after about six months, but the perpetrators were not found. Instead a patrol of two Carabinieri in a jeep has been stationed in front of the building ever since.

Sometimes, as I study the medals of our old landlord Pope Paul V, I fantasize that he is sitting in the very room where I am working and he has kindly granted me an interview. I would like to ask, as tenant to landlord, a couple of questions. For instance: *Which of your exploits are you most proud of?* I imagine he might say that he was proudest of his Acqua Paola aqueduct.

There is another question, a more tricky one, that I might dare to ask if I could find a way of doing it with delicacy: *Could you tell me about some of the medals you chose not to make?* My studies have shown that Paul was far more than a planner and a builder of great palaces. He was a mover and a shaker in matters of religious orthodoxy as well, and in 1603, when he was still a cardinal, he was known to hold very strong (some said antiquated) views about papal supremacy and was named as Inquisitor. When he became pope he began to press for absolute papal control in the

Italian states, but stubborn Venice, having forbidden the acquisition of land by the Church without permission, refused to submit. Enraged, Paul tried to win obedience but when Venice stood firm he placed them under a papal interdict. In the end King Henry IV of France intervened and forced Paul to withdraw his interdict – a move which clearly embarrassed the Pope.

From this time onward, Paul was more cautious in ordering states to yield to Vatican control. But he did not hesitate to condemn individual citizens. On one historic occasion in March 1616 he censured Italy's foremost scientist, Galileo Galilei, for teaching the Copernican theory of the solar system – and the whole matter of the Copernican treatise was put on the Index of prohibited material 'until corrected'.

But since I don't dare mention Galileo, I have thought of making it a more innocent question. For instance: *What do you think will be your place in Italian history?* I suspect that the Pope, being clever at public relations, might give me a very Italian response. 'I am quite serene about my reputation,' he might say. And then, 'The people always respected my abilities as a churchman and as a builder. They trusted me to take care of them. I built their great basilica of St Peter's after so many popes failed. I brought them fresh drinking water from the country.

'My predecessors were not as prudent as I was. Think of my namesake Paul IV. He was a man of great learning, but he was also a harsh Inquisitor. He was suspicious of the Jews, fearing that they were secretly abetting the Protestants, so he confined them strictly to the Ghetto and made them wear special hats. He took on as a cardinal and adviser his worthless nephew Carlo. So when he died, the people exploded with joy. They rushed to destroy the headquarters of the Inquisition and released all the prisoners, and then they stormed up to the Campidoglio [Capitoline Hill] where they knocked the statue of Paul IV off its plinth and chopped it in pieces.

'I look back upon my reign with great satisfaction. No one has ever torn down my statues. My name is there for all to see on the façade at St Peter's, the greatest church in Christendom. And I am buried in state in a beautiful chapel of my own design in Santa Maria Maggiore. When visitors come to pay homage at my tomb, they come with esteem and reverence. What more can any pope ask?'

CHAPTER NINETEEN

The Tax Office Shuffle

ACCORDING TO A LEADING FRENCH SOCIOLOGIST, 'A STRONG and independent bureaucracy is a fundamental part of any real democracy.' To the casual visitor it would appear that Italy, bound in a permanent knot of red tape, has a strong bureaucracy. But I suspect that the opposite is closer to the truth. 'Weak bureaucracies are the result of weak governments,' wrote another sage, and it is a fact that, Italian governments are always weak, made up of unstable coalitions that are permanently subject to blackmail by the smaller coalition partners. The apparently solid left-wing Prodi government, which took over after the Tangentopoli (Bribesville) scandals in 1996, was torpedoed by one very small party of splinter communists. And even Silvio Berlusconi, who likes to act the strongman, is in constant terror that his patched-together coalition could be torpedoed at any time by the xenophobic Northern League, which has less than 4 per cent of the national vote. Its leader, Umberto Bossi, caused the first Berlusconi government to fall in 1995 after seven months in office, and he often threatens to do it again.

From this it follows that the politicians, feeling insecure, are only happy when surrounded by weak bureaucrats, who will back them through thick and thin. These Yes-men and -women in the various ministries know that their main job is to please the minister and his clients, and so they forget about their obligations to the public and spend their days performing an odd little pantomime, where they appear to be very busy but in reality are doing nothing. This is the good old Tax Office Shuffle. They snap to attention only when some higher-up in the office happens to pass by.

We were given a front-row seat to watch the Tax Office Shuffle soon after we moved into our flat, when we discovered, to our surprise, that the big stone building directly across the street from our bedroom window was the home of a major government office. The building is a rather grim stone edifice, four storeys high, bristling with undercuts and large chunks of decorative masonry that project a foot over the pavement, posing a serious threat to people with wide shoulders or long necks. Since we kept our bedroom windows curtained, we had the impression at first that no one lived in the building because there was little visible activity during the day and no lights in the evening. One night, several months after we'd moved in, I was jolted awake at 5 a.m. by a strong shaft of light that swept right across our bed.

'Burglars,' I whispered, pounding on Robert's shoulder.

Once awake, we crept to the window and pushed

back the curtain, to find the light originated from a room directly across from us on the third floor. Two Filipinos in green overalls were busy cleaning the floor and dusting piles of folders stacked from floor to ceiling along the back wall. The room was a large office.

Next morning we went to have a closer look at the building, and discovered a small plaque next to the door which said 'Ufficio Generale delle Tasse di Roma'. We were living right next to the main tax office for the city!

'*Mamma mia*,' I murmured, 'that's all we need. A tax office right across from our bedroom, and a church across from that!'

'It's a good sign,' Robert said, extending the index and little fingers of his right hand (a gesture to ward off evil spirits and other unpleasant things). 'We are surrounded by symbols of death and taxes. But they are too close, they will never notice us.' And in fact they never did.

The idea that we were sleeping within whispering

distance of a major Italian tax authority caused some of our Italian friends to shiver, but I prefer to think of it as a learning experience. It gave us an insight into the way the tax office worked and an overview of the whole landscape of Italian bureaucracy − a study far more educational than a vista of the Roman forum or the dome of St Peter's.

One would expect that those in charge of collecting taxes in a prosperous city like Rome would be people with a certain moral rigour. Since these are the folk who keep a record of the incomes and expenses of the citizens they have a position of considerable power. They can find out how much people pay for their maids and doctors and new computers, and they hold a life-and-death grip on thousands of purses. One would expect them to work with diligence and honesty and trust them to treat all citizens equally. But are they really worthy of that trust? Let us see.

The official hours for government employees in Rome, who comprise the biggest single group of workers in the city, are established by law. They must come in at 8 a.m. and they are supposed to work un-interruptedly from then until 2 p.m. six days a week. This makes a six-hour day with afternoons pleasantly free, which should add up to a working week of thirty-six hours − not overly demanding. However, Saturday is regarded as optional by all but the most timorous government employees, so their working week in truth dwindles to only thirty hours.

We decided to conduct a discreet survey to see how closely the tax collectors were abiding by this law. The following morning at eight o'clock I pulled up a chair behind the thin curtains at our bedroom window. On my first day I learned some surprising things about the work habits at the tax office.

It was like a scene from Gogol. The office was empty as a tomb at eight o'clock. I expected some action by eight thirty but nothing stirred. I went to the kitchen to have tea and toast. At nine the first worker appeared wearing his topcoat. He took off the coat and put it on the back of his chair, and laid his briefcase on the desk. He studied the mass of files stacked against the wall, and after a brief hesitation he extracted about a dozen bulging folders and arranged them artistically around his briefcase. Then he pulled out his car keys and headed for the door. It was clear that he was going to move his car, perhaps to a better parking spot – or perhaps he had another appointment (or another job?) in a different part of town.

At nine thirty two or three workers wandered in holding paper cups of *caffellatte* and at ten o'clock I counted eight workers in all. Ten minutes later there were five more, a total of thirteen. In Italy thirteen is a lucky number. But they did not appear to be doing very much work. Half of them settled down comfortably to read newspapers, while the others appeared to be engaged in friendly banter from one desk to the next. Probably they'll get down to work later in the morning, I thought hopefully.

I checked in at different times from eleven o'clock until two to try to judge the intensity of the work, but I discovered that from eleven o'clock until one the number of people in the room actually *diminished* by nearly 50 per cent. And this happened twice. At

eleven thirty the thirteen tax workers had dwindled to
only six. Three of them were still reading newspapers
and three were playing cards. Where had the others
gone? They were back to a full complement when the
twelve-o'clock cannon went off, but this was only
temporary. By twelve fifteen the number had dropped
down to six again.

It eventually became clear that our neighbours had
worked out a rota system so that everyone had an hour
off in the morning to enjoy a cappuccino and a bun,
and to do their household shopping at the open market
on Piazza Monte d'Oro. (We were to learn later that
women workers were also granted an eighty-minute
break once a week to go to the hairdresser con-
veniently located across the street. The chief stylist
himself confided to me that his morning schedule was
completely booked up by the ladies of the tax office.)

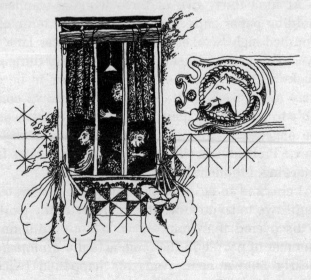

Proof of the market visits appeared at eleven thirty each morning when plastic bags began to sprout from the bars of the office window facing us. These bags contained perishable goods like chickens, milk, lamb chops and fresh fruit and vegetables, and on Fridays salt cod that the fishmongers had soaked overnight in brine. Hanging these purchases out of the window kept them fresh, and had the added advantage of making the telltale bags invisible from the interior in the unlikely event that a government inspector should drop by.

At about twelve forty-five the valiant tax workers began to collect their goods from the window ledges and to fold their newspapers into their briefcases, and by one thirty the office was virtually empty. It would remain unoccupied until the Filipino cleaners arrived at 5 a.m.

This early departure gave the tax officials plenty of time to drive home (they all came to work by car and parked illegally in front of their building), partake of an abundant lunch in the bosom of the family and possibly have a nap. After the nap it has been estimated that fully 50 per cent of Rome's bureaucrats go off to work at other well-paid jobs in the private sector. (Both our plumber and our electrician can come to us only in the afternoons, as they work for the Ministry of the Navy in the morning.) Thus when evening came and we repaired to our bedroom there was no need to pull the curtains because the office was deserted; there were no spies watching to see if we were hiding gold bullion under our mattresses.

'You know a funny thing,' I said to Robert recently.

'There are two things missing in that tax office.'

'What are those?'

'There are no telephones and no computers.'

'Huh,' Robert replied. 'You know why they have no telephones? Because they don't want to talk to the public. Banks don't have telephones either.'

'But what about the computers?' I asked. 'I read in the papers that the government had bought a whole lot of new computers from Olivetti, but they're not using them.'

'Why not?' said Robert.

'Maybe because most of the workers in that office have been there for twenty years. They are too old to have been trained on computers but they are protected by law so they can't be fired. As long as they hang on to their jobs, nobody with computer skills can be hired to replace them.'

How could any government tolerate such a situation? Easy. There have been nearly sixty changes of government in Italy since the Republic was formed, so new ministers have no time to focus on bureaucratic reform before their term is over. Their main interest is simply to cling on to power (the chauffeur-driven limo, the free plane and train tickets, etc.) as long as possible.

Members of the public, for their part, clearly prefer to have a tax office with no telephones and no computers. They also prefer a police department where the officers turn a blind eye to triple parking, and where the rule about seat belts is universally ignored.

This aversion to authority is widespread. Farmers hate the government, and so do accountants. The late

Gianni Agnelli, head of Fiat, Italy's biggest motor manufacturer, put it neatly in an interview. 'I think there is a lot to be said for a weak government in a country like Italy,' he said. And the little fellow feels the same way. Having suffered under all kinds of despotic regimes (both foreign and papal) throughout history, the Italians long ago decided that the only people they could trust were members of their own family or special groups of loyal friends (the Mafia being one of the extreme examples).

Everyone hoped for a better deal when a new republican form of government emerged after the Allied victory in 1945, but when the Marshall Plan was set up to help with post-war reconstruction the Americans made it quite clear that no assistance would go to any communist government. So the conservative political forces in Italy who called themselves the Christian Democrats remained in power for fifty years with the approval of the Vatican and the American government, and the tacit support of various minority parties, chief among them the Socialists. This extra-long clutch on the reins of power inevitably brought corruption and complacency.

The small print in the Christian Democrats' contract with the voters reads, 'We'll take care of you as best we can. We'll make safe jobs for many of you in the government offices where you can never be fired. You'll also get free health care, pensions for life and maternity leave, and we won't be too tough about taxes. All we ask in return is that you don't complain, and pledge to vote for us at the next election.'

This agreement continued for roughly a half century,

until it was rudely interrupted by the near-bankruptcy of the government in the early 1990s, accompanied by the Tangentopoli bribery scandals, which resulted in the virtual disappearance of the entire Christian Democratic party. A power vacuum developed as large as the crater of Vesuvius. This vacuum was filled in an amazingly short time by a brand new power group called Forza Italia (Long Live Italy!), organized and financed entirely by the richest man in the land, Silvio Berlusconi. In 1994 Berlusconi got himself elected Prime Minister, despite the fact that he controlled the biggest private television network in Italy, and had a number of criminal charges pending against him for cooking his books and bribing judges. The fact that he made only a token attempt to resolve his blatant conflict of interest didn't seem to bother the new Prime Minister at all, although it brought heavy and repeated protests from his European Union neighbours.

The Italians switched their allegiance to the new powers that be, and they still look to government as a Great Golden Beehive, the source of virtually all the wealth in the land. There are two ways to tap into this honey. One is to burrow inside the hive, by getting yourself elected as a deputy or a senator or a member of a regional council. Once elected, you can devote your energy to organizing grand schemes for government spending, like roads, new government buildings, defence equipment and bridges (the gigantic bridge to Sicily is an example). All such schemes require *appalti* (contracts) for billions of euros. This is where the biggest bribe money can be made. (A new underground rail link recently built in Milan cost double what a similar railway cost in Berlin.) Another method is to capitalize on whatever connections you have to people inside the hive, to find yourself a posh job in the bureaucracy, with good working hours, plenty of benefits and an assured future with a splendid pension.

If you are not lucky enough to get inside the Great Golden Beehive, your only other option is to try to cut down on the money that you contribute to it. Tax dodging has always been, and still is, endemic to the Italian way of life and this skimming operation is one of the most flourishing enterprises in the land, which explains why almost no one complains when the workers at the tax offices spend most of the morning buying food for the family or going to the hairdresser.

Here is a list of the rules that govern bureaucratic behaviour in Italy, given to me by a journalist friend:

The Ten Commandments for Model Bureaucrats
The citizen has no rights whatsoever.
1 Refuse whenever possible to receive any petitioner who wants to see you.
2 Deny at all times that you have any competence in the matter that interests him.
3 Never grant any request the first time you receive it. Always make the petitioner come back at least once bearing a document that he failed to bring the first time.
4 If someone forces you to grant some request, make it clear that you are doing it as a special favour, and you could just as easily have refused it.

5 Never be clear or unequivocal in your communications to anyone. Ambiguity is your strongest weapon.

6 Apply the law with cold logic to all citizens whom you regard with indifference. Interpret the law positively for friends and negatively for enemies.

7 If possible, never show your face or give your name so your decisions can never be blamed on you personally.

8 Never take any responsibility for any decisions you make; always impute all responsibility to your superior.

9 The more obscure a rule is, the better it is. That enables you to make elastic or sliding interpretations that will never get you into trouble.

10 Never reveal the personal identity of any higher-ups who have power in your office. That tends to weaken their authority, and consequently it weakens your authority too.

I believe many Italians are born with these rules encoded in their DNA.

CHAPTER TWENTY

Antonio di Pietro: The Rise and Fall of a Good Man

THE ANCIENT ROMANS WERE AMONG THE GREAT LAW-makers of history, but somehow they never managed to solve one crucial problem: how to find good men to administer the laws they made. In Italy, where many of the Western world's laws originated, it has always been difficult to find honest men and women who are willing to sacrifice their own personal ambitions to work for the benefit of the nation.

Too often Italy's history has been decided by tyrants intent on increasing their own imperial power, or by itchy-fingered politicians who are concerned not with the public weal but with consolidating their own positions as richly paid members of the privileged ruling clique. Thus the arrival out of the blue of a courageous man who seemed determined to rid Italy of its chronic corruption stirred and excited ordinary Italians as they had not been stirred for generations. The man's name was Antonio di Pietro. He was an unlikely hero, to say the least, and the story of his success and subsequent downfall is one that throws a disconcerting light on the condition of democracy in Italy today.

I first saw Di Pietro on television back in 1992. He
was a countryman from the backward south, and a
leading magistrate in the Mani Pulite anti-corruption
campaign in Milan. He, more than any other single
person, managed to expose and partly destroy the
blanket of corruption that had smothered Italy's
Christian Democratic government for fifty years. When
he and his colleagues had finished their investi-
gations, the Christian Democratic party and their
partners the Craxi Socialist party lay in ruins, and
dozens of other corrupt bribe-takers, influence-
peddlers and plain conmen were sent to jail or driven
from the political scene. It looked as if Italy, with a
fresh new leftist government, might for the first time
in fifty years shed its image as the most corrupt
country in Europe.

Antonio di Pietro, who had the husky build of a
heavyweight boxer, certainly did not look or act like
most of his fellow 'substitute procurators', who
function in Italy rather like district attorneys in the
USA or special prosecutors in England. He came from
the Molise, a dusty downtrodden province in the
south where clever farm boys went straight from
school into the Carabinieri, and he tended to speak in
quick staccato tones like a man in a hurry, using
homely country phrases instead of political clichés.

When he spoke of his enemies who were conspiring
to destroy him with a campaign of dirty tricks, Di
Pietro cited 'corvi che mi girono sulla testa' (crows
who are flying around my head). And when he spoke
of disgraced politicians who were trying to clear their
names and reputations when they got out of jail, he

accused them of trying to '*rifarsi la verginità*' (remake their virginity). But behind the rustic façade there was another quality to Di Pietro that won him a place in the hearts of ordinary Italians: he never kowtowed to people in authority; he never credited them with titles such as *onorevole* or *cavaliere.*

Italians are not used to this kind of audacity, especially from their poor cousins from the south. They treat politicians as if they are royalty, keeping their eyes cast low when they meet. I will never forget one electrifying morning back in 1992 when the RAI began to televise the Mani Pulite hearings from the Milan courthouse and Di Pietro, as chief prosecutor, put the Honourable Bettino Craxi on the witness stand. Craxi, the head of the Italian Socialist party and a long-time Prime Minister, was accused of accepting millions of dollars' worth of bribes in cash, many of which were carted to his office on Milan's cathedral square in paper bags. A politician of monumental self-esteem, Craxi was used to being treated as a demigod. Di Pietro, still an unknown figure on the TV screen, stood up, pulled awkwardly at his black toga, and looked the politician straight in the eye.

'Your name?'

Craxi looked as startled as if he had been struck.

'Bettino Craxi!'

'And what do you do?' Di Pietro asked. Craxi's answer was lost as a murmur of disbelief swept through the courtroom. People were not accustomed to seeing their potentates treated in this fashion.

At that precise moment I knew that Di Pietro was the fearless man I had been looking for, the man who might finally bring something good to Italy. Thousands of Italians watching this plain-spoken ex-police officer had the same reaction, and in very short order Antonio di Pietro became the most admired man in Italy. A thumping 72 per cent of the citizens said that he was the person they admired most in the country.

The story of Di Pietro's rise to power is in itself an extraordinary one for an Italian. Though he was born poor, he had a countryman's deep yearning for fairness. He hated watching strong and powerful people pushing the weak around.

He acquired some special abilities not often shared by young men starting off in the traditional way in the Carabinieri: he became a whiz at electronics and computers. This passion had developed when he was very young, and even as he was making his first arrests as a city cop Di Pietro spent much of his spare time studying the new computer systems. In the end he earned the title of *perito elettronico*, which means he had reached the top level as an expert on electronics.

By the early Eighties he was promoted to the rank of Commissioner of Police in the Milan area, and went to work breaking rings of car thieves who operated around the airport. In this period he also managed to crack open a corrupt system of 'easy drivers' licences' that had existed in the Milan motor registry for years. Here for the first time Di Pietro put his computer skills to work sniffing out and then solving a crime.

What he did was to ask the motor vehicle department of Milan to give him the names of all the people who had received licences from their office in the last five years. When the answer came back there were

800,000 licences granted. Di Pietro knew he could never put all these names on his very primitive computer so he asked the motor department to tell him the names of all the people who lived in the provinces but had gone to Milan to take their driving tests. The answer was 78,000 people. He next asked the motor people to look separately at the towns near Milan and find out how many licences had been issued for each town each year, and of these what proportion were Milan-issued. Eventually Di Pietro discovered that, in the town of Ardesio in the Val Seriana region, of the 210 people who had acquired licences in a given period 150 of them had made the trip to Milan rather than being tested at home. A goodly number! What had brought so many Ardesians to Milan?

Di Pietro got the names of twenty of these Ardesians and summoned them to report to his office all at the same hour of the same day, so that the twenty could see each other without being able to speak. Wearing his best Commissioner's uniform, he walked into the waiting room where the twenty nervous Ardesian drivers were assembled. He shuffled a sheaf of official papers.

'*Buon giorno*,' he said to the crowd. 'Now I want to talk to you one by one about how you got your driving licences and who gave you your tests.'

The first two people he questioned claimed nervously that they had received their licences after legitimate tests, but they could not remember where they had been tested, or by whom. By the time he turned to the third driver, the others could see that the game was up and confessed. In the end all twenty people admitted that they had paid bribes for their licences, thus enriching the examiners and also putting a lot of untested and possibly dangerous drivers on the roads.

Di Pietro repeated this process for the rest of the Milan area. In the end he arrested sixty examiners from the motor department for taking bribes, and another forty employees of the driving schools who were in on the racket.

Soon after this triumph, in the mid-Eighties, Di Pietro won a public competition and moved from the police department to the office of Procurator for the Department of Justice. From policeman to Carabiniere to prosecuting attorney in only a few years. The country boy from the Molise was on his way!

Di Pietro recalls that he felt like a fish out of water when he moved into the austere offices of the Chief Procurator, Francesco Severio Borelli, in the Milan courthouse.

'I was very isolated,' he says, 'because I didn't know anyone: and when I talked to people in the office I tended to use country Italian, to mix up my words; I still do. I wasn't good at social relations either; I wasn't invited to supper at any of my colleagues' houses. I was the only one who addressed Chief Prosecutor Borelli using the formal *Lei* instead of *Tu*. I didn't play tennis. I didn't belong to a club.'

The Milan office was in the doldrums when Di Pietro arrived. The magistrates worked independently, he recalls, and all they ever got for their troubles were '*schiaffi e schiaffi*' (slaps and slaps and more slaps) from the appeal judges who ruled on their cases. The

frustrated attorneys knew that the laws were inadequate; they needed new rules and new techniques to investigate the system of political kickbacks and *tangenti* (bribes) that dominated political life. But the ruling government did not seem anxious to hand them more investigative tools.

To track down the system of bribes for favours that characterized relations between politicians and big businessmen in the Milan area (and eventually throughout Italy), Di Pietro decided to use his computers to seek out money that had been hidden in offshore bank accounts, and was therefore quite possibly *soldi neri* (illegal or dirty money). To find this hidden money Di Pietro sent Carabinieri to most of the major government agencies in Milan, asking them to supply all their bills and contracts for 'consultation' with private firms that had their headquarters abroad. Once he had these documents, he told his computer people to pull out all the bills which ended in more than five zeros.

Why five zeros? Because Di Pietro reasoned that if a government office ordered a large supply of nails or bolts from Singapore, and people in Singapore sent a bill for 509,674 lire, the deal could well be legal. But if a private company, with headquarters in Liechtenstein, paid a large sum such as 8,000,000 lire to a government office for 'consultation fees', the payment could be a bribe. Fiat came to confess early on, as did other leading industrialists such as Carlo di Benedetti and the leaders of the electrical company Enimont. They all admitted that they had paid out bribes with offshore funds, always, they claimed, because they were pressured to do so by politicians. Di Pietro told them that if they co-operated with the government prosecutors and gave the names of the politicians they bribed, they would not go to jail. Instead they would be obliged to pay large fines and give back any illegal money. By doing this, he told them, they could save their businesses from ruin, while the politicians would get caught. Only one big entrepreneur refused to cooperate. Silvio Berlusconi, Italy's richest man, fought back from the very first, screaming that he was innocent, the victim of a communist plot.

The Di Pietro system worked and within only a few years the political clique that had run Italy for fifty years was in tatters. The numbers do not really show the enormity of this change but, as Di Pietro says, the Mani Pulite campaign revealed only the tip of the iceberg. After winning a number of key convictions, Di Pietro's luck started to dry up. This was because a new political coalition was forming to take the place of the fallen Christian Democrats, and the man who was heading this new group was none other than his old enemy, 'Cavaliere' Silvio Berlusconi, who realized that the only way to escape the serious bribery charges against him and save his tottering empire was to be elected to government himself. He took power in 1994. His government lasted seven months. (Berlusconi's closest ally, Bettino Craxi, saved his own skin by ignominiously fleeing the country and retiring to his luxurious seaside villa in Tunis.)

The Cavaliere recognized that Di Pietro represented an enormous threat to his financial and political ambitions, for the young magistrate was not only extremely popular but had an office full of floppy disks that could quite possibly sink the entire Berlusconi empire. So he planned a two-fold attack. First he telephoned Di Pietro from the Quirinale office of the then President, Oscar Luigi Scalfaro, to offer him the key post of Justice Minister in his new Berlusconi government. Di Pietro turned him down. Simultaneously, according to Di Pietro, Berlusconi set his lawyer, Cesare Previte, to work hunting up material from Di Pietro's past to discredit him. The sharks were gathering in the torpid waters of Italian politics or, as Di Pietro put it, the campaign of '*killeraggio*' (killing) against him picked up steam. His enemies were powerful people and to increase his clout Berlusconi had in his employ platoons of newsmen working for his three TV networks, and newspaper columnists who were prepared to publish anything Berlusconi said and repeat it day after day until the public began to believe it. The lawyer, Previte, came up with a couple of pals from Di Pietro's Carabinieri days who were prepared to claim under oath that they had lent him money, or had given him a Mercedes car. In the end ten cases against Di Pietro were sent to trial through a Mafia connection in Sicily whom Di Pietro had incriminated years before.

Di Pietro recognized that the crows were indeed flying around his head, until he finally removed his toga in public and resigned. To the bafflement of his admirers he never explained why he was resigning and his supporters began to worry. What had happened to their hero? Was there some unsavoury reason why he gave up so quickly? Was he perhaps, as his opponents suggested, planning to take advantage of his enormous popularity to launch his own political career?

Di Pietro has been asked this question over and over again, but finally (after he had been cleared of all charges pending against him) he granted an interview in January 2002 in which he gave his answer: he left because of the circling crows.

It turned out that there were twenty-seven charges in all against Di Pietro, covering everything from corruption to collusion, abuse of office, attempts on the Constitution, false ideology and even sexual harassment of a female journalist (the lady herself took the stand to deny the charge). Di Pietro fought the charges one by one, a 'calvary of four long and bitter years' as he put it, during which time he made no speeches and gave no interviews and the Berlusconi-owned press engaged in a merciless campaign of vilification against him. But in the end he was exonerated. The judges, and there were dozens of them, ruled that the accusations against him were a trumped-up pack of lies.

As Di Pietro described it, 'If I had been accused of murder it was as if all the judges had said, "There is no case here. The dead man is still alive."'

Once he had cleared his name, Di Pietro did go into politics and became a senator in the left-leaning coalition. He found out to his dismay, however, that the members of the coalition spent most of their energy fighting each other and not their political foe, the right-wing leader Silvio Berlusconi. His left-wing allies also tended to keep Di Pietro at a distance, some because they thought he used strong-arm techniques as a government investigator, others because the savage publicity campaign against him had cast a shadow over his name. The strain of what he had been through was beginning to show, and when Berlusconi flunkeys taunted him for his political ambitions and the collapse of his anti-corruption campaign he became almost speechless with rage. Some observers said he was starting to look like a man on the verge of a breakdown.

In a RAI chat show, organized to discuss the tenth anniversary of the Mani Pulite campaign in 2002, Di Pietro found himself once again alone facing a panel of eight bitter enemies. Four of these were former politicians whose careers he had ruined and who wished him dead. Four more were obedient vassals from Berlusconi's Forza Italia party who had orders to go for the jugular. Eight against one. The RAI appeared to have stacked the deck deliberately against the former prosecutor. Di Pietro should never have allowed himself to be cornered in this manner, and he defended himself as bravely as he could. But one man is no match for a group of eight enemies and the more he tried to explain himself the louder they shouted insults, until no one else on the programme could be heard. Desperate, he flipped through his thick sheaf of papers to find some document he needed and the papers slipped to the ground in a miserable heap.

In the end, Di Pietro came away with a few small triumphs. One was when Craxi's daughter, who has been waging a campaign to restore her father's reputation, looked straight at Di Pietro and accused him of having killed her father, who died 'in exile' in Tunisia. Di Pietro looked back at her, 'cold as ice'. 'Craxi didn't die in exile,' he said. 'He died in Tunisia as a fugitive from justice.' The old prosecutor had not lost his spark.

But still I felt a sense of outrage. It seemed clear to me that Di Pietro had been left out alone in the cold. Mani Pulite had boomeranged.

But my sadness was perhaps premature.

Within a week of the chat show, a group of liberal intellectuals, together with film director Nanni Moretti and the Nobel Prize-winning actor Dario Fo, invited Di Pietro himself to attend a demonstration in Milan to celebrate the tenth anniversary of his great campaign. It was a cold Sunday afternoon in February, a nice time to sit cosily at home and read the newspapers, but the word got around and people came in droves, about 40,000 of them in all. They came by car or bus or train to join the protest and to argue that Mani Pulite and the work of Tonino di Pietro had not been in vain.

'A lot of us have false teeth and hearing aids,' said one of the chief speakers. 'We're hardly revolutionaries. But we feel that our freedom is endangered; it is time to restore the rule of law in Italy, and get rid of politicians who are thinking not of Italy but of their own skins.'

Cameras showed an overflow crowd standing in the piazza in front of the hall. Suddenly a tall man who looked like a prizefighter found a workman's ladder and leaned it against a wall so he could climb up onto a wobbly iron platform that surrounded the arena. Clutching a megaphone, the man began to speak.

'My fellow Italians,' he began, '*benvenuti*. I am glad so many of you have come this afternoon to speak out against the new corruptors and to support the principle that all Italians, great and small, rich and poor, are equal before the law.'

It was Antonio di Pietro, small-town boy from the Molise, policeman, Carabinieri officer, chief prosecutor, enemy of graft. With his usual torrent of words and fractured grammar, Tonino seemed back in control again and the crowds cheered him on as he had not been cheered in years.

'Bravo, Tonino!' they shouted. 'Keep up the good fight!' It seemed as if the wind might be blowing from a different direction at last.

CHAPTER TWENTY-ONE

Gabby the Gabbiano's Aerial Circus

WHENEVER THE POLITICAL WINDS BLOWING AROUND US got too stressful we enjoyed retreating to the quieter world of our terrace, where we could watch the birds going through their aerial gymnastics.

We knew them all quite well by now: the swallows with their joyful swoops and swirls, the blackbirds who perched on the television antennas to give their evening concerts and the resident pigeons who achieved unexpected prosperity when Via Veneto fell out of fashion and the cafés in the nearby Piazza in Lucina became newly chic. The pigeons generally roosted on the roof of the building facing our terrace and in the mornings they flew straight over to the piazza to pick up the crumbs and crusts dropped by the early morning crowd who came for *caffe latte* (coffee with milk) or *caffe corretto* (coffee 'corrected' with a shot of grappa). At noon and again in the evening they often managed to make off with some peanuts or potato crisps left by customers who dawdled over their aperitifs. We even smiled ruefully when a couple of stray crows flew in to bully the

pigeons: I don't think the crows actually attacked
the pigeons but they had a way of sitting up on the
chimney pots and staring down at them with such a
fixed gaze that the pigeons became nervous. We could
only wonder what the crows meant by this menacing
behaviour.

But the worst was yet to come. Just at the time when
Rome began getting ready for the Millennium celebra-
tions, a new and far noisier group of birds started
appearing in our peaceful back alley – seagulls. Even
now, two years after the Jubilee, they are still with us.
The leader of this invasion is a frantic female gull
whom I have named Gabby the Gabbiano (*gabbiano* is
Italian for seagull) who fills the air with her laments.
Her range includes everything from a raucous croaking
noise to a loud catlike meowing, and from the bark of
an angry dog to a booming machine-gun screech.
When very excited, Gabby can even bray like a
donkey. Until her arrival, the back piazza offered a
charming lifestyle to the local birds. Now it is no
longer *their* piazza; in fact many of our birds have gone
away, and the brave pigeons who remain have been
driven off the rooftop and now cling anxiously to little
fixtures in the wall that hold back the shutters. Since
these fixtures are so small the pigeons can only get a
grip on them with one foot, and have to flap their
wings to keep their balance. To add to their troubles,
they shiver and hop around nervously every time
Gabby squawks, but they can almost never see her
because she is hidden by the roof ledge. Poor pigeons.
It is Gabby's piazza now and we have all become the
spectators of her daily dramas of overburdened

motherhood, shrieking babies and treacherous and unreliable male gulls.

The Gabby invasion was not altogether unexpected. Although we had become accustomed to watching the seagulls assembling alongside the Ponte Cavour on the Tiber, only a block from our flat, we had long been led to believe that seagulls would never leave the water for the terraces of Rome. Then one evening we were having dinner on a terrace above the Campo Marzio when a large flock of seagulls appeared overhead, flying southward in a determined fashion. Suddenly two of the group dropped out of formation and landed on the dome of the Pantheon.

I was shocked. 'What are those gulls doing landing on the Pantheon?' I asked.

A fellow diner who knew about birds assured me that this was most unusual behaviour. The two gulls were probably just tired, he said, and would soon rejoin their squadron, which was now on its way to a recently opened rubbish tip south of Rome.

'They are scavengers,' he said, 'and the only thing that interests them is new garbage. They are absolutely not city dwellers.'

A year passed, and then one night we were awakened by a great cacophony overhead, and looked out to find a flock of seagulls, possibly as many as twenty birds, wheeling and screaming over the church roof. In the morning when I took tea on my terrace I saw a large white-headed herring gull perched on the chimney across the alley.

We did not make eye contact as I was determined to ignore it, hoping the bird would go away. But a few days later, when a gang of Albanian builders started to throw up scaffolding just below the chimney, I heard one builder yelling an alarm to his mates. He was waving a large pole in the air, trying to swat a screaming seagull who kept swooping down like a bomber pilot to take a swipe at his uncovered head. When the excitement had dampened, the man informed me in broken Italian that the seagull had made a nest next to the chimney out of lemon peelings and old plastic bags, and that in the nest there was one seagull egg, spotted brown and white.

The need to incubate this treasure seemed to be Gabby's sole preoccupation, but she made it clear in strident tones that she needed help. She sat on the egg in such a way that she was always facing in the direction of the Tiber, and for hours she would direct her fury and reproach towards the seagulls on the river. Eventually two or three huge gulls (males, I assumed) came swooping in from the west, making several deep passes at the nest, screaming all the time, before flying away. It was obvious that Gabby was expecting food, or even some relief on the egg-watch, but as far as I could see none of the male gulls offered assistance of any kind. (This despite the statement in our bird encyclopedia that 'both gull parents incubate the eggs and tend the young'.) The encyclopedia also offered the chilling information that gulls are very gregarious, usually nesting in large colonies. Gull eggs, the book said, take up to thirty-three days to hatch, and after that it is six weeks before the young birds fly. That means the mother bird has to be on duty for at least seventy-five fun-filled days. *Santo cielo!*

We had already made plans to go to New York for the month of June 2001 so we were absent for the hatching, but when we got back to Rome in July we found the situation on the nearby roof had deteriorated. Gabby's egg had hatched all right and had produced an enormous baby, all brown and white spots, who was nearly as big as his mother; his only interest was to follow her around, head bent low in supplication, shrieking for food with a high piercing whistle that penetrated the bone like a fire alarm. He seemed able to produce this whistle continuously for two or three hours without even opening his beak. On the second day back we realized there were not one but two of these whistlers on the roof. If you add two whistlers to the constant screams of two or three mothers, plus the shrieks from various peripatetic males, you end up with a barrage of noise that does not diminish as darkness falls but increases in volume as the night wears on. Gulls apparently do not need sleep.

We are therefore hatching a plan whereby we will go down every night after the El Toula restaurant closes and scatter the bags of rubbish over the alley, so that the scavenging gulls on the roof can spot it. Then, we figure, the gulls will get organized to make a mass attack on the garbage collectors (just as they attacked Tippi Hedren in Hitchcock's *The Birds*), so the collectors will refuse to come into the alley unless the gulls are removed. Or, alternatively, they will come to their job each night equipped with catapults (or dare I say shotguns?) until the gull population is eliminated. Then our sleep will have only one interruption per night: the ungodly crash of discarded bottles as they land in the sanitation department's iron truck. Surely one crash in the night is better than the squawking of a hundred semi-hysterical seagulls?

Even as we were trying to cope with the gulls above us, articles began to appear in the newspapers about far worse seagull behaviour in other parts of Rome. In midsummer a birdwatcher wrote to *La Repubblica* that nearly every day at dawn he was witness to bloody aerial battles in the skies above the Palazzo Barberini. Screaming squadrons of seagulls attacked passing pigeons, he claimed, generally killing one or two a day and terrifying hundreds of others. The pigeons were beginning to realize, he went on, that they were no longer the undisputed kings of central Rome. These seagulls were described as '*una novità assoluta*' (complete novelty) in Rome. There was speculation as to how the *gabbiano reale*, who in nature invariably nests close to the seashore, had found his way to the rooftops of the city.

An answer came immediately from an impeccable source. Fulco Pratesi, president of the Italian World Wildlife Federation, wrote that it was possible he was personally responsible for this new breed of inner-city gull. In tones reminiscent of early Darwinians, he blamed the invasion on one single mutation, or perhaps it would be more scientific to call it one 'single accident' happening to one single female gull.

This story, published in August 2002, relates that back in 1971 some Roman bird-lover brought to his studio a female gull who was missing a wing after a bad accident (it was possible that she had hit a power line). The bird was kept until the wound had healed, and then, knowing that she could not survive in the wild, her rescuer took her to live in the sea-lion cage around a cement pool at the Rome zoo. Sea lions apparently have no taste for seagulls, so despite the missing wing and the fact that she could not fly, the gull prospered, and even exerted a 'certain fascina- tion' for passing male gulls. In time she produced a number of healthy baby gulls, who thrived on the zoo diet of fresh sardines and tiny animals born in the pool such as goldfish, frogs and lizards. The baby seagulls did not mind the hard cement of the pool. To them it was as warm and friendly as any rocky cliff over- looking the sea. Eventually some of the young gulls flew up to the umbrella pines above the pool because they felt safer up there, and in time they built nests in the pines so they too could start families. But once their eggs were hatched they stayed in the zoo area, where they could get fresh sardines and other sea-lion handouts. As the offspring of a disabled bird, they remained forever innocent of the call of the deep blue sea or the seagull colonies that lined the islands and shores of the Mediterranean. All these things could be taught to them only by seagull mothers but their mother was unable to do so because she could not fly.

Over time the gulls around the zoo became thoroughly citified and began to make their nests with the materials they found nearby, items like discarded paper handkerchiefs, picnic wrappings or even the plastic covers of soft drinks cans. This ability to adapt apparently gave birth to a whole new breed of city

gulls, who became, like many immigrants to big cities, adept at finding new food sources and scrounging what they liked from the urban environment.

The zoo was where it all began, according to the article, but some time later a large gull colony was discovered by workers who were replacing a tile roof on the Corso Vittorio, and later a big colony was found on the roof of the Chiesa di Gesù near the Piazza Argentina. Another was found on the top-floor attic of the Palazzo Mattei. The conclusion was drawn that 'today Rome is the only city in the world where Royal Gulls nest on rooftops, far from their usual nesting place on distant islands or rocks and lonely caves on the edges of the sea'.

This is a charming story but frankly I am sceptical, for my research shows that for a number of years colonies of roof-nesting, citified seagulls have been reported in cities as far apart as Trieste and Naples. Back in 1999, journalist Christopher Emsden spotted a fellow who was climbing around the rooftops of Trieste with a notebook and camera in hand, and discovered that he was an experimental psychologist named Fabrizio Antonelli, who was earning a degree studying the special behaviour of seagulls making new homes and new lives on the rooftops of both Trieste and Venice. According to Antonelli, these gulls were beginning to act very much like cats, with whom, he said, 'they appeared destined for a Darwinian showdown'.

Antonelli claimed that the new 'immigrant' gulls were extremely clever, and awesomely adaptable. They regularly devoured snacks left outside for stray cats, they knocked on people's windows and they showed unusual skill in hanging around near fish stalls at seaside markets in the hope of handouts. New items on their diet were chicken bones and feet, prosciutto, pizza, stale biscuits and fruit and vegetables. They had also shown, to nearly everyone's delight, a taste for rats.

As the city gulls gain confidence, they are learning new tricks every day. The World Wildlife people from Brescia have revealed that when the city opened its Montichiari airport in 1998, they were seriously troubled by the fact that three huge flocks of gulls used to fly in at nine every morning and leave at 5 p.m. on the dot, causing a hazard to aircraft. A study revealed that the gulls had memorized the working hours of the airport dump, which opened at nine and closed at five.

They're getting cleverer all the time, the psychologist Antonelli thinks, and also meaner; in fact his research indicates that a new class of warrior seagulls is emerging. The birds in our neighbourhood are already terrorized and it may be that the gulls' next victim will be our local alley cat. This tough feline, the Duke, had our back alley all organized, with the cat-catcher coming round every morning at nine to feed him. The Duke got a shock not long ago when a squadron of seagulls swooped down at nine on the dot and made off with his breakfast. Sandra the *gattara* waved her knapsack at the gulls in vain, and the Duke darted underneath a car parked in the alley and hasn't been seen since.

CHAPTER TWENTY-TWO

Our Jubilee Terrace under Attack

WHENEVER LIFE GETS DULL IN ROME, THE POWERS THAT be dream up some new carnival or celebration to stir things up again. We had already been subjected to one Holy Year, one Second Vatican Council, one Summer Olympics and a couple of world soccer championships. But the carnival they dreamed up for the year 2000 was the mother of all carnivals – the Vatican-backed Jubilee, when millions of pilgrims, the biggest crowds ever, were expected to flock to Rome to celebrate two thousand years of Christianity.

The previous events had taken their toll but it was the Jubilee, when Rome was converted into a building site, that really did us in. Actually, Robert and I had planned to spend a good part of the Jubilee Year away from Rome, so when 1999 began we looked to the future with considerable calm. We had enjoyed a couple of years of relative peace in our terraced flat, and despite the invasion of seagulls we had no major household worries. The leaks onto Signora Scarpa's oriental rug had apparently ceased. The watering system was working well, and it appeared that the terrace was settling down into a bright and comfortable old age where we could enjoy the sun and air without becoming too involved in the chaos below.

But then came a miserable Monday in April 1999 when we received a depressing letter from our landlord, La Cattolica, telling us that the Mayor of Rome had decreed that all the major palazzi of Rome should be repainted to celebrate the Jubilee. We should prepare ourselves for the erection of scaffolding some time in the summer to 'facilitate the circulation of the painters'. The letter went on to point out that our apartment was especially important to the operation because it contained the only third-floor terrace in the building that could be used as a 'level space' on which to assemble some of the painting equipment that would be lifted up from the Vicolo di San Biagio. For this reason, the letter concluded, we should begin to clear all the plants off our terrace so that operations could begin, 'possibly in the month of August'.

We did not answer La Cattolica's letter. Two months later the front doorbell rang, and I found myself confronting a sturdy Sardinian *muratore* (mason) wearing a paper hat, who introduced himself formally as Capo Maestro of the Millennium Squad. He wanted to know if we were removing the plants from our terrace.

'No, we are not,' I said.

'But you are obliged.'

'I may be obliged but I'm not going to remove anything. I've removed our pots already three times.'

'But, signora, this is the Millennium!'

'I don't care if it's the end of the world.'

'But what can we do about your plants?'

'Do what you want. Put them on the roof. Put them anywhere at all, but you cannot expect us to move our plants again.'

We heard no more and it seemed that the battle had been won. Apparently La Cattolica had decided not to go ahead with the painting project in the immediate future. Even if the job were to be done eventually, it seemed clear that nothing would happen before mid-August or September, so we felt free to go ahead with our plans to spend three weeks of July in the Hamptons. We had arranged to swap our flat in Rome with a house belonging to friends in Sag Harbor. We didn't want to worry our friends so we told them that if any builders appeared at our front door while we were gone, they should not let them in.

After two weeks of sailing and swimming in Sag Harbor we got an e-mail:

> The doorbell rang yesterday morning and a fellow in a paper hat asked us if he could see the terrace. We told him we were not authorized to let anyone in so he went away. But today there are two trucks parked just below the dining room window and the men are unloading armloads of pipes and bolts which look very much like the raw material for a scaffolding. What should we do? Yours, Pete

We e-mailed back:

> Don't let anyone in, and don't worry.

Three days later we got another communication:

We aren't worrying, but workers in the back alley are starting to place supports for a scaffolding, and it is clear they are going to surround the entire building with walkways. What should we do? Yours, Pete

We e-mailed back:

We are very sorry. We thought this was not going to happen. Keep us posted.

The next day came the clincher:

Today the scaffolding has climbed up past the first floor and is getting higher every hour. We figure that within three days they will have reached our windows. Then we will be under siege. We have just called Alitalia, and they say they can get us out on a plane on Thursday, so we think we will advance our departure if you don't mind. We have had a lovely time in Rome, but scaffolding is more than we bargained for. Pete.

We e-mailed back that we too would advance our departure and would probably cross them in mid-Atlantic.

Eventually, after a late-night arrival, we were back in our flat. After noting the presence of a spider's web of pipes outside our palazzo we fell into bed. Around eight thirty I was awakened by voices, and saw two smiling faces, wrapped in the folded paper hats of the Roman *muratore*, peering in through my open window.

'Yahoo,' said one, who had a big gap in his front teeth.

'What are you doing in my bedroom?' I asked.

'*Noi muratori,*' said one with a strong non-Italian accent.

'*Salve,*' said the other.

I groped for a dressing gown and closed the window. Then I went to find the Capo Maestro, who was standing on our terrace talking earnestly to Robert.

'There are two men in our bedroom,' I said, 'and they don't even speak Italian.'

'Some Albanians, some Bulgarians. We have all of Eastern Europe on this job,' replied the Maestro.

'You mean you are doing essential Jubilee work with illegal labour?'

The foreman looked unconcerned. 'We tried to get Italians but they are all away at the beach and won't be back until September. Jubilee can't wait. All the buildings in Rome have clandestine workers, even the Vaticano.'

'But have you tried—?' I began.

'I don't give a *fico secco* [dried fig],' he interrupted. 'If I don't get Italian workers, I get fined. And if I don't finish the job on time, I get fined too. It's all the same to me.'

Robert waved his hand at me. 'I've explained the whole thing to my friend Gigi here,' he said. 'I told him we've moved the plants three times already and he realizes that we simply cannot move anything again, so he has promised to try and work around the plants.'

I looked at my shattered terrace. All my pots had

been detached from their watering tubes and shoved into the corners to make room for a big block-and-tackle construction to raise equipment from the street to the terrace. Even as I watched, a worker unloaded two buckets of cement, which was being used to plug holes in the stucco walls. He looked around for a place to put down a bucket, but since the floor was occupied he balanced it precariously on top of my biggest lemon-tree pot.

'He has to scrape down all the imperfections in the wall first, before it can be painted,' Robert said.

'And when will they actually start painting?'

'Who knows?' replied the Maestro. 'First, we bring up a lot of wooden boards so that we can make a walkway in the scaffolding. The painters need space for their paint cans.' He cast me a nervous glance. 'That means you'll have to close all your windows and all the *persiane* [shutters] too.'

I began to protest, but Robert interrupted. 'Look, honey, there is nothing we can do,' he said. 'These guys have a job to do and they did warn us. We did leave the pots here. So Gigi will do the best he can. He'll have the men put some of the biggest pots on the walkways, and he promises to see that they get watered every evening. After all, we still have a hose out here.'

The next day, to our infinite relief, Gina took over the problem of the workers. She rolled up all the rugs in the house and wrapped them in heavy paper. Then she collected all the family silver and wrapped the pieces one by one in cloth and stowed them in our only large cupboard with a padlock. She wrapped up

Robert's statues too, along with our favourite paintings.

Then, only after the family treasures were secure, she ventured out to have a few words with the Capo Maestro. I was not present at this conference but it seemed to have a beneficial effect because the next day he greeted me when I came out to survey the terrace.

'Good morning, signora,' he said with a near-smile. 'I have just been talking to Gina here and I think we have worked out a solution to your problems. She says that you have a house in the country not far away. I suggest that you go there as soon as possible, thus relieving yourselves of all the *impicci* of this operation, and leave Gina to take care of your interests.'

The suggestion seemed like a good one so we packed our bags and departed for Canale, leaving our *tuttofare* in charge.

We received almost daily progress reports from Gina. For the first week she told us the workers were bringing their materials up to our terrace and getting the scaffolding in place. The blinds were closed so very little light filtered in, although there were a few rays of daylight in the kitchen. Speaking of the kitchen, Gina explained that the Maestro had a mild liver condition that meant he needed a cooked lunch every day, and she would be happy to provide this in the interests of good relations.

During the second week, Gina reported that the workers were now involved in preparing the building for its coat of paint.

'They can't help it,' she told us, 'but the air is full of flying powder all day, and it gets into the apartment

even though I keep all the windows tightly closed. But don't worry, I will give everything a good cleaning when the job is done.'

The next week the painting was supposed to start and I expected it would all be finished in ten days. But hitches developed, as they do in Italy. Gigi could not go ahead until he got an OK on the colour of the paint from the Ministero delle Belle Arti.

'The ministry is getting lots of complaints that the buildings of Rome are being painted the wrong colour,' Gina told us. 'They want them all to look alike for the Jubilee. So now Gigi has painted four different sample colours on the front wall of the palazzo, so that an assistant minister can come to choose the one he wants. But the assistant has not come all week.' The assistant didn't come during the second week either, but at the end of the third week, when everyone's nerves were reportedly *a pezzi* (in pieces), the minister came and chose a colour that Gina said reminded her of peach sherbet.

Work resumed in the fourth week with only a few minor mishaps. One dust-up occurred when a Bulgarian painter fell asleep during his noon rest hour, and woke up to find a Romanian painter calling his girlfriend in Bucharest on the Bulgarian's mobile phone. The Bulgarian raised a fuss that nearly exploded into fisticuffs, but the Romanian explained that by mistake he had picked up the Bulgarian's phone, which was green, while his was a pale shade of grey. He thereupon gave his grey phone to the Bulgarian, who used it at once to call his mother in Sofia.

Then there was the problem with the girls who were restoring the church opposite. As Gina explained to us on the telephone, a group of very pretty girls, all art students, had appeared on the scaffolding on the Chiesa del Divino Amore to restore the mosaics of the bell tower, which had fallen into disrepair over the years. These girls were from upper-class families but they were not immune to the calls from our *clandestini* resident painters, and after several days of chatting across the alley two of the youngest and best-looking of the Romanians took off on their lunch hour and climbed up onto the church scaffolding to get better acquainted. They carried a bottle of wine with them, and the girls produced some paper cups. The party seemed to be going well until several nuns appeared on the terrace to hang out the laundry, and immediately started protesting that the visitors should return at once to their side of the alley. When the painters showed no sign of departing, the nuns began to wave wet towels in their direction and threatened to call the *parroco* (parish priest) himself. Eventually, with great reluctance, the Romanians bid the girls goodbye and clambered down off the church roof. As they resumed their places on our scaffolding their fellow *clandestini* gave them a muffled cheer of support. It isn't often that *clandestini* have much to cheer about in Italy,

Eventually Gina reported that the building was painted and the workers had finished. We returned at once, and as we drove towards Piazza Borghese we realized that the city of Rome, repainted in gentle pastel tones for the Jubilee, had taken on the aspect of a tutti-frutti stage set.

Gina had cleaned up our apartment until it shone

but the terrace looked as if it had been hit by a cyclone. At least half of the plants were dead, having been overlooked in the infrequent watering sessions, and many more showed signs of serious battering. Our biggest and best lemon tree, for instance, had lost all but one frail branch, from which sprouted only a few tattered leaves. The second lemon tree was looking poorly and several of its strongest branches appeared to have been smashed from above, possibly by falling scaffolding; but Robert noted that five or six green lemons were clinging to its lower branches, which indicated that the tree's vital juices were still flowing. Our two dark red oleanders had also survived the chaos, but this was not surprising as the oleander, a true survivor, can be seen blooming happily alongside miles and miles of Italian autostradas, where it is rarely watered. I know one stretch of brilliant pink and crimson oleander bushes that leads from the town centre at Sperlonga down to the beach, a distance of some 700 metres, and I have never seen anyone watering them in all the years I have trodden this rocky path.

We noted sadly that all our geranium plants, some of which had survived for six or eight years, had given up the ghost. Geraniums need a lot of water. Also gone were most of our roses, which do not appreciate being left unattended in a hot climate. But there were survivors among my collection of edible herbs. I was delighted to find that a couple of rosemary plants, essential for roasting chicken and lamb, were growing well. Another culinary herb, the silver lavender, was also flourishing after recent neglect. Indeed, my big silver bush, the result of a cutting that Lord Lambton had given me from his kitchen garden at Centinale, had not only grown in size but was making a few silver-blue flowers. Another rather delicate lavender, *Lavandula dentata*, was also flowering handsomely.

Even though our supply of plants seemed to have been cut in half, we went to work moving our pots back to the edges of the terrace. La Cattolica had brought in a new rule that we could no longer put plants on top of our terrace wall because the pots, once watered, tended to dribble and would ruin the freshly painted walls.

'I'm afraid it will look very bare with nothing on top of the wall,' I commented as Robert shoved the bigger pots into place.

'No, it doesn't look so bad,' Robert said, stepping back. 'In fact, I think it's almost an improvement.'

I knew that he was just trying to make me feel better, but I stood to have a longer view.

'You may be right,' I said. 'It does look very spacious. I mean, you would hardly guess what the poor terrace has been through.'

With the pots removed from the top of the wall, the terrace seemed to have opened up. Instead of a nearly solid screen of shrubbery and flowers that had effectively blocked the view, we could now look out to see other rooftops and also the blue of the sky, which gave our terrace a new dimension. Since the remaining plants now had more space around them, it was possible to appreciate their unique forms and colours as individuals, and not as mere elements in a wider tapestry. I was impressed by one colour that had previously escaped me on the terrace, and this was the pale grey of the lavenders, which gave it a decidedly Mediterranean tone. The grey also provided contrast with the pinks and blues of the smaller bedding plants, especially the petunias and snapdragons that grow so well on Roman terraces.

'Yes, you really are right,' I said to Robert after a moment's hesitation. 'I would never admit this to anyone but you, but it needed drastic pruning, and now that it's been pruned it's beautiful.'

'Less is more,' Robert said with some solemnity.

Viva il Giubileo.

CHAPTER TWENTY-THREE

Envoi

WHEN THE JUBILEE YEAR ENDED WE TRUSTED THAT LIFE in Rome would return to normal. The buildings were brighter, the piazzas had been polished, and the gardens were full of extravagant blooms. To achieve this transformation the city had been turned into a year-long construction site that frayed nerves, but once it was finished we had to admit that it had gone better than expected. Jubilees weren't so horrendous after all.

And then, in spring 2000, we became aware of a new threat from an unexpected quarter – the sky. Suddenly, on a quiet Saturday morning in May, we noticed a giant green crane slowly rising skyward from just behind the tax office across the street. The crane rose to about six storeys high, and then a large transversal arm was lifted up by a pulley system and attached to the top of the pole by a crane operator who had climbed up the rigging.

Once he had completed the hook-up, he hauled himself into the operator's cabin and hung out a canvas flag bearing the company name. Then he switched on the motor. Gradually, like a mammoth praying mantis, the arm of the crane moved above the roof of the tax office, swung over the newly polished bell tower of the Chiesa del Divino Amore and paused, aiming directly at our terrace.

'Look,' I said to Robert. 'Our terrace is being attacked by a big green *gru* [crane]. It looks like it's going to bite.'

Once it was pointing in our direction, however, the crane arm hovered in the air, its menacing finger as stationary as an oversized traffic beacon. Our local seagulls, who are nothing if not observant, began to show an interest in the huge iron 'tree' that towered over the surrounding rooftops. Some of the more adventurous gulls started perching along the arm as it gave them a commanding view of the neighbourhood, and particularly the rooftop near us where the female gulls were sitting on their eggs. Our friend Gabby the Gabbiano had returned for a second season, with three other female gulls who made nests near her. All this nesting activity attracted much attention in the bird world. Several large hooded crows, who used to be occasional visitors, came by almost every day, to perch on television antennas and peer down at the gull nests in a menacing fashion, but Gabby and her friends were quick to fly up and scare them away. One crow lost his bearings in flight and ended up only a few feet from a nest, but Gabby put herself between the nest and the crow and then opened her large beak only inches from the crow's head, a threatening gesture that sent the marauder off in a hurry.

Just before sunset the big male seagulls would fly in from the river to settle on the crane one by one. Their

seating arrangements were almost as fussy as those for a
dinner party at Buckingham Palace. If one gull
happened to land closer than a metre from his neighbour, the neighbour would immediately fly off and
choose a more isolated position on the crane. By sunset
there were usually twenty to thirty seagulls parked on
the crane; they spent the rest of the night keeping watch
on the nestlings and chattering back and forth with the
females. Some of these conversations started with a low
mewing sound, but once the gulls got excited their
voices grew louder until they sounded like horses
whinnying. This hubbub went on for hours, making
sleep difficult. Our alley had become a seagull stadium.

One morning after shopping I ventured behind the
tax office to find out where the crane had been
planted, and eventually I found it tucked into the big
garden that surrounds the Palazzo di Firenze, home of
the Dante Alighieri Society. There the green monster
stands huge and motionless next to a magnolia tree,
one-time home of blackbirds. Nobody in the area
seems to know who dumped the *gru* in the garden or
why. From one angle it appears to be positioned to
take the roof off the tax office, but who would want
to do that? Or it may be preparing to do some major
work on the church opposite our terrace; but it seems
foolish to use a six-storey crane to repair a small building barely one storey high.

After brooding about the matter for some weeks I
dreamed that the crane was actually a listening tube
installed by some mysterious secret service. This
organization wanted to keep a closer watch on the
residents of our area, and had established a system

designed to inform the powers that be of what the citizens of central Rome were up to.

We are a motley crew, we denizens of central Rome, and over the years we have witnessed hundreds of changes and grappled with a thousand calamities. We have seen Rome struggling back to life after a long and costly war. We have lived through the Anni di Piombo ('years of lead' when the Red Brigades held Rome in terror). We have seen it change from a sleepy village, where nearly all the faces on the street were familiar, to a hectic metropolis invaded by thousands of buses, motorcycles and cars. We have now reached the point where something has to give. The streets of Rome, built for walking and small chariots, have been taken over by an army of vehicles that fills every inch of every street and every alley, and when they have blocked the streets completely they double and triple park even on the pavements and in building entrances.

The politicians seem to think they can cope with all this by passing more laws, and I have been told that there are more laws on the books of Italy than of any other developed country. But once the law is passed, and the politicians have taken their obligatory bows on TV, nothing happens. Like the monkeys who cannot see or hear or speak, Italian bureaucrats are more concerned with other things, like safeguarding their own jobs or getting ready for their second (black-market) job in the afternoon. As a result the law about seat belts has been universally ignored for many years, as has the law forbidding the use of mobile phones while driving. There is a sign forbidding parking on the street in front of our palazzo, for instance, but the area has been parked solidly for years, and I have never seen anyone getting a ticket.

This total lack of enforcement makes life even more perilous for pedestrians, who are obliged to walk in the streets because the pavements are blocked. The aim of the traffic laws is to speed up the traffic, not to protect walkers. Thus there are very few zebra crossings, and those that exist are frequently worn out and nearly invisible. Traffic lights that offer help to pedestrians are as rare as traffic policemen. The chaotic street corner at the Ponte di Cavour near us is supposed to be controlled by a special officer wearing high-visibility braces, but whenever I look for him he has taken off his braces and is hiding behind the awning of the riverside café overlooking the corner. Angry snarl-ups are continuous. The Via del Corso, for instance, in the heart of old Rome, was sealed off years ago to make it a pedestrian walkway, but now private cars bullet down it in a constant stream as if it were Indianapolis. I have teetered at the edge of a zebra crossing trying to get across the Corso for as long as five minutes while drivers blithely zip past me. Eventually, when some polite motorist takes pity, I creep forward with caution because there is a 50 per cent chance that two mad motorcyclists lurking on the far side of the driver will zoom forward into what I thought was a safe zone, threatening me with instant death.

Going down narrow streets where there is no pavement is another trauma for people on foot, especially those carrying baskets. Most Roman drivers, if they see someone walking down a narrow alley, will speed up

deliberately rather than honking, to frighten the pedestrian into getting out of the way. They barrel past at top speed and if the poor pedestrian lacks the agility to paste himself against a building he may end up without his basket or even with a broken leg.

This indifference to the public weal has been the characteristic attitude of the ruling classes in Italy since the sack of Rome in May 1597. Whether the rulers have been authoritarian aristocrats, corrupt and oppressive popes, foreign rulers from Spain, France or Austria or dictators like Mussolini, the citizens have learned to keep their heads low. And since they have never experienced a democratic system, they have for centuries survived by huddling with their families or clans for mutual protection. Sociologists, who like to label societies, refer to today's Italy as 'pseudo feudal or tribal'. To Italians the state has always been the enemy, and although they have developed clever systems for tipping their hats to the bosses (whoever they may be) and grabbing what the state may offer them free, they have never given their deep allegiance to any group beyond the family. There may have been a period after the Second World War when many Italians, both workers and intellectuals, were lured by the egalitarian promises of communism, but with the collapse of the Berlin Wall this dream of a world of justice and freedom vanished.

Now the insidious lure of American-style consumerism has grabbed them, and a newly prosperous class of small entrepreneurs compete with each other to see how many smart cars they can cram into their garage, and how many TV sets and computer games they can set up in their children's bedrooms. These newly prosperous Italians have little sense of civic cohesion or loyalty; as one wag put it, young Italian men do not want to go out and die on the battlefields for noble ideas; they would rather die smashing up their Alfa Romeos on the nation's highways.

Indro Montanelli, one of Italy's most respected journalists and a sage for most of the twentieth century, died in 2001 at the age of ninety-two, despairing that his beloved Italy could ever achieve a workable system of democracy. 'I have given up hope,' he said in *Indro Montanelli: Only a Journalist*. In this book, Montanelli wrote of the great disappointments that his country had caused him during his long career. He spoke of the repeated moments, especially immediately after the Second World War, when Italian statesmen were hammering out a constitution and appeared set to establish a bipolar system of democratic government. But on each occasion the system collapsed because of friction between power-grabbers in the splintered parties. Few politicians were willing to abandon their personal hopes and ambitions in favour of the collective effort needed to make a bipolar system of government work. Or, as the old saw has it, everyone in Italy wants to be a chief and nobody wants to be an Indian.

'I have come to the conclusion,' Montanelli wrote, 'that bipolarism is not possible in Italy because it goes against the genetic code of the Italians . . . because of our vocation of always looking at everything in our lives from the point of view of our *own particular needs*' (as opposed to the needs of the whole group).

'We carry this gene in our bloodstream and there is no way on earth that it can be extirpated.'

He went on to quote from a father of Italian juris-prudence: 'In this country reforms are not only useless, but damaging, because they always lead to something worse. In Italy there is no need to reform the electoral system, nor the laws, nor the rules. There is a need to reform the Italians.'

Montanelli, who considered himself a conservative, admitted frankly that the last great delusion of his long life came with the failure of the Mani Pulite campaign. 'With few exceptions, all of the politicians who were caught believed in a double morality: one for the Prince and the other for his subjects . . . and the thing that enthused the Italian people was that here finally was a battle between a group of good judges and a gang of rotten politicians. It was impossible not to support Di Pietro . . .'

Montanelli went on to suggest, however, that Di Pietro's colleagues at the Milan procurator's office made a mistake in giving him the leading role of St George fighting the dragon. 'To be the chief witness of a great cleansing "baptism" like this one, it was not enough to have *mani pulite*,' he said. 'One had to be absolutely immaculate in every way. Di Pietro was not a dishonest man. He was an excellent policeman, very able in extracting confessions and questioning witnesses, but he was *uno sventato* [rather reckless]. And he was not always careful in his choice of acquaintances. I think his colleagues made a mistake in trying to turn this very able policeman into a Robespierre. They should have known that his defects would ultimately emerge.'

In one of his last weekly television appearances, Montanelli was asked to talk about the future of Italy. The journalist took a deep sigh. 'As you know, I have lost the hope that the Italians will get together to make themselves a truly democratic state. Italians have never had any feelings for their national identity . . . They have been surviving for a long time on lies and fabrications and ancient myths and now they are sick even of lies.'

But then Montanelli's lean face lit up with a conspiratorial smile and he edged his long frame forward in his chair. 'I believe that the only hope for Italy in the future remains with the European Union,' he said. 'That is a strong organization which could play an important role in the development of a democratic Italian state.'

Montanelli expressed the hope that the EU might also take suitable action to break the monopoly grasp that Prime Minister Berlusconi has fixed on Italy's television news.

'But if this doesn't happen,' he went on, 'you know what I would wish for the future? I would like the European Union to take over the government of Italy. I would like the Germans to control the Ministry of Finance. I would like the French to take over the bureaucracy, and the British to administer the Justice Department, and maybe the Scandinavians to handle the national health service. We could bring in the Swiss and let them worry about taxes.'

I was never sure, after this programme finished, whether Montanelli had been serious or not. But in his penultimate TV appearance, the great journalist went out of his way to point out that although he despaired of much in Italy, he had a high opinion of many of its individual citizens.

'I believe that individual Italians are among the most creative people on earth,' he said. 'Think of the honours they have won in the fields of science, art, literature and even economics. They are enormously intelligent. They are hard workers. They have excellent taste, and make wonderful designers whether they are designing concert halls or museums or ladies' handbags. But you will notice that many of the best of them win their honours after they have left Italy and gone abroad.

'There is something about Italy that seems to hold them back. It may be that Italy does not encourage collective efforts. There is little sense of community participation here. Too much depends on who you know, and not what you are worth. It is a nation of individualists, and joint endeavours always seem to end in squabbles.'

In his concluding statement he made note of the fact that he had just turned ninety-two: 'Despite the great good fortune I have had in my life,' he said, 'I am afraid that it is my destiny to take with me to the tomb the two things I have most loved: my profession of journalist and my country. The demise of journalism is now clear for all to see. But to renounce my country is a sacrifice I could never make, although I understand that it is necessary and even inevitable. I can only thank the march of time that will exclude me from any decision.'

Montanelli loved to play the merchant of doom and he seemed to take a perverse satisfaction in announcing that his life had been a failure and that every cause he had supported had ended in ruins. But I suspect there was something else in his make-up that he could not hide no matter how he tried, and this was a kind of desperate, buoyant hope that Italians would one day see the light.

For throughout his long career, which began when he was sent by the United Press as a young journalist to cover Ethiopia, he never abandoned his single-minded search to find the answers. He travelled everywhere and met many of the world's movers and shakers. He was on a first-name basis with kings and queens, prime ministers and presidents, but there is no gossip in his books, no boasting about scoops he made or famous actresses he fancied; his writing was simply a long and often bitter chronicle of his endless search for a brighter and better Italy.

And no matter what he said, his hope and enthusiasm never left him. Even when he was in his eighties he got out his umbrella and walked across Milan in the rain to stand outside the court building waiting for the latest news in the Mani Pulite case.

Even in the last weeks of his life, he was still hunting for new solutions for his beloved Italy, a nation that includes among its citizens a surprising number of passionate and committed individuals (like himself) who occasionally stop grumbling, and look about with the hope and creative imagination that have always been part of the heritage of Italy.

Maybe some time soon they'll find a way.

Bibliography

Abate, Tiziano, *Indro Montanelli: Soltanto un Giornalista*, Rizzoli, Milan, 2002.

Coffin, David, *Gardens and Gardening in Papal Rome*, Princeton, 1991.

Howard, Lelia Caetani: Pittrice e Giardiniera, catalogue of paintings, Carlo Virgilio Gallery, Rome, 2001.

Jacob, Lauren, 'The Medals of Paul V: An Exploration of Papal Identity', in *The Medal*, British Art Medal Trust, 2002.

Kelly, J. N. D. (ed.), *Oxford Dictionary of Popes*, Oxford University, 1996.

'Perché ha Vinto il Centro-destra', Italian National Election Studies, Società Editrice il Mulino, Bologna, 2001.

Valentini, Giovanni, *Antonio di Pietro: Intervista su Tangentopoli,* Laterza, Bari, 2000.

Veltri, Elio, and Travaglio, Marco, *L'Odore dei Soldi,* Editori Ruiniti, Rome, 2001.

NOTES FROM AN ITALIAN GARDEN
Joan Marble

'THIS DESCRIPTION OF MAKING HEAVEN ON EARTH IS
AN UNLOOKED-FOR DELIGHT'
Independent on Sunday

*'I fell in love with Etruria one chilly evening in January. They
were having a New Year's Eve festival in a little town near
Campagnano, and a group of local boys dressed in Renaissance
costumes were marching in a torchlight parade down the
main street. As I stood there in the cold watching the flames
lurching to the sky, I realized that I felt very much at home in
this ancient place. If ever we should decide to move to the
country, this was the kind of place I would choose . . .'*

Thirty years ago Joan Marble and her sculptor husband Robert
Cook bought a piece of unpromising land in Lazio, the area
north of Rome that was home to the ancient Etruscans. They
built a house and, more importantly, grew a wonderful garden.
The challenge was both exciting and daunting, and poor soil,
an inhospitable climate and the blank incomprehension of
their neighbours sometimes made it seem as though they
would never realize their dream. But Joan and Robert's
enthusiasm for the land, their determination and inspiration,
and the unexpected friends who helped them, all served to
make the landscape blossom.

'THIS BOOK IS ALL ADVENTURE. MS MARBLE DOES
SOME DIZZY TRAVELLING. HER ROOF BLOWS OFF. SHE
SURVIVES KILLER WASPS AND POISONOUS PINE MOTHS.
MOST INSPIRING OF ALL SHE REVIVES A WILTING
CLIMBER WITH TWO CUPS OF COLD RICE PUDDING AND
TAKES GERMINATING SEEDS TO DINNER PARTIES. I WISH
I KNEW HER. I LOVE HER BOOK'
Phyllida Law

'A STORY OF A HOME CREATED WITH LOVE AND
PASSION. EVEN NON-GARDENERS WILL FIND IT
ENCHANTING'
Irish News

0 552 99841 9

BLACK SWAN